Métisse

Yvonne Combs

MÉTISSE by Yvonne Combs
Published by Creation House
A Strang Company
600 Rinehart Road
Lake Mary, Florida 32746
www.creationhouse.com

Previously published ISBN 0-9772215-0-4.

Cover design by Terry Clifton

Library of Congress Control Number: 2007924902
International Standard Book Number: 978-1-59979-199-9

First Edition

07 08 09 10 11 — 987654321

Printed in the United States of America

Dedication

I would like to dedicate this book to our Lord, who has given me wings. Thank You, Lord, for using me for Your glory.

I also dedicate this book to:

My beloved mother Gioi Thi Truong, who gave me root.

My husband Charlie, a veteran of three wars and a survivor of a forty-five-month internment in a Japanese prisoner-of-war camp. This dedication also includes the veterans of all services who have so gallantly defended this "land of the free and home of the brave."

My beloved son Chris, who is now with his heavenly family. I am so grateful to have had a loving son like you. I love you and I am always with you.

Acknowledgments

I wish to first thank God for giving me life. He bequeathed my life through my mother and father. I also thank God for giving me wisdom and guidance. With faith I have completed this task through many hours of toil and concentration.

I would also like to express my deepest gratitude to my mother, who brought me into this world and has loved, shaped, and guided me throughout my life. I love you very, very much, Mother. Thank you, Mother, again for giving me root.

To my father, it seems like we have been separated for a long time. I hope that you will be happy when you finish reading this book. Please don't feel bad or guilty because of what happened in Indochina. Be proud of your daughter, because if you had never been in Vietnam, I would not have had the opportunity to write this book. I thank you for trying to find me. Through our strong faiths we have found one another. I love you and have missed you all my life.

My thanks also go to my half sister and my half brother for accepting me into your lives. We will also cherish our father's memories.

To my husband Charlie, I thank you for always being there for me from the day you said, "I do." Through the good and bad, sickness and health, we have traveled the road together, sharing our load side by side "until death do us part." I love you, Charlie.

To my son Christopher, I thank you for loving me and being my son. I love you very much and always will. You are in my heart for now and all eternity. The sunshine you brought each day will remain in memories.

I thank God for giving me three precious grandchildren—Samantha, Amanda, and Vanessa—who bring the sweetness into my life. Grandma loves you very much, and you can count on me to be there for you whenever you need me.

To Tom Lamberson, thank you for your help, but most of all I thank you for not violating my morality and burying my principles. I will never forget your departing words: "Good luck in America."

I would like to acknowledge Mr. Bob Hope and his troop of entertainers, who helped the morale of the soldiers while they were thousands of miles away from home. The songs that he sang certainly helped to heal their wounds after a long day of fighting out on the battlefields. Some soldiers might say, "Maybe we might not come back or ever have the chance to see home again after this field trip, but we are very proud to be American soldiers."

My thanks to the staff at Strang Communications and Creation House for their work on this book: Tessie DeVore, Allen Quain, Virginia Maxwell, Atalie Anderson, and Dinah Wallace.

My thanks also go out to all the readers of my book.

Thank you to the doctors and the rest of the staff at the VA Hospital in Gainesville, Florida, for their excellent surgery and care for my husband in July 1996. Thank you to Jonnie Willis, Sharon Pace, and Wilford Harrison from the DAV.

On behalf of myself and the people of Citrus County, Florida, I would like to express my thanks to Governor Lawton Chiles, the entire staff from FEMA, the Salvation Army, and the American Red Cross for their help which enabled us to survive the "No Name Storm," on March 13, 1993. Through our misfortunes, some of us have gained newfound friends. I would like to print the names of everyone who helped with the "No Name Storm."

Lynn Mansfield, McEven, IN
Pat Reynolds, Colorado Springs, CO
Darlene Theophilus, Mt. Vernon, OH

Catherine Konick, Arlington, IL
Floyd Baveom, Kansas City, MO
Nelson and Ruth Gritten, Kalamazoo, MI
Genevieve (Genny) Sheridan, Baton Rouge, LA
Maggie Whelan, Festus, MO
Nina Ritter, Saginaw, MI
Marie Espinoza, Waynesville, MO
Norman Volden, Orlando, FL
Robbie Fehrenback, Panama City, FL
Brian Barron, Central Panhandle chapter
Stephanie Bass, Mountain Hope AFB, ID
Sean Kassebaum, Mountain Hope AFB, ID
Veeda Rowen, Colorado Springs, CO
Wally Webhoelter, Overland Park, KS
John L. Harper, Inverness, FL
Peggy Veal, Port Richmond, CA
P. J. McCrary, Middleburg, FL
Georgia Maxwell, Crofton, MD
Karen Yescas, Linden, CA
Julian Firanti, Citrus Springs, FL
Lesha Cowart, Meridan, MS
Loretta Malin, Clio, MI
Charles Daniels, Creve Coeur, MO
Louise Boggs, Easley, SC
Jan Mock, Strongville, OH
Bon Carnley, Panama City, FL
John Wilson, Phelps, NY
Barbara Moshier, Gulfport, FL
Mary Snell, Huntsville, AL
Aurora Bolding, Olympia, WA

Contents

Prologue		viii
1	Métisse	1
2	The Love Story Begins	3
3	The Consequences of Being a Métisse	14
4	A Beautiful Bud Unbloomed	24
5	In the Danger Zone	41
6	A Dream Comes True	59
7	A Promise	66
8	Return to the Motherland	73
9	The Shadow of My Beloved	90
10	The Pursuit of Happiness	124
11	The Land of the Morning Calm	133
12	A Family's Chaos	141
13	The Reunion	152
14	God, Please Give Me Strength	167
15	Mother's Thirty-Six Days of Faith	180
16	Come to Christ	198
Epilogue		213

Prologue

The French Footprint

From my firsthand observation as a child who knew war but no peace, I can tell you that it is always the ones who are left behind who suffer the most and continue to suffer long after the conflict is ended. I often wonder what the wars in Vietnam have accomplished.

Looking back for a moment on my mother's life, I realized that the war had captured her youth, and her life was shared with the shadow of darkness when the French footprint became embedded in her land. In 1947 she married a man she never knew, fully aware of the fact that separation would soon follow. A Vietnamese wedding was performed in the church, but proper documentation was not available because he was a married man. When this man's military duty ended in this land, her marriage also ended; and her *j'attendrai* song began.

Many buds of flowers had no chance to bloom in those days of war. Mother's hair had not been tangled with any dust of life. She was twenty years old. In 1948, when this man departed on the ship, he left her behind with a heart in despair; like the rose leaf that falls, it lost its color and died. The bud of beauty bore the fruit of pain when she gave birth to her baby girl. A new chapter began. Would her baby girl arrive at her destination?

This baby girl was baptized when she was one month old in a Catholic church. Outside that same church the baby girl would someday find her only protection in a statue of the Virgin Mary when other children abused her. She inherited a new name, *Métisse*, meaning "half-breed." Unfortunately this child tasted a bitter life at a very early age.

To me war is just one of many human failures and is likely to remain with us for years to come. Most people will agree that war is useless and senseless; yet many will also agree that, at times, war is necessary, and they will even support it. What a dichotomy! In my opinion war has three phases: cause, acts or actions, and consequences.

Historians explain the conduct of war very succinctly. Once war starts, both sides just muddle through until the most determined side wins. The cost in human lives, the misery, and the abhorrent economic losses are beyond most people's comprehension if they have not witnessed war.

The consequences are almost never far ranging in terms of human history. We need only to look back for the last two thousand years to see this. I would think that Jesus Christ had a far greater influence upon all societies than any war. Perhaps World War II had a greater consequence for all the world society than any other war. At the end of that terrible conflict, the United States set out to rebuild Germany and Japan, using the Marshall Plan in Europe. As we can see today, the plan was successful.

I believe that there are some good things that come from war. I would not have been born if there had never been an Indochina War. My father was French and my mother was Vietnamese. I could not speak Vietnamese until I was six years old and the French had left Vietnam. So, but for the French in Indochina, I would not be sitting here now writing this significant story of my life. I have often wondered if these events were fate or merely chance. Suppose I had not been born during the war. Suppose the French had never come to Indochina. The *ifs* in our lives are often borne from regret to make excuses for what we have attempted but failed to achieve.

Please share with me through the following pages the experiences of my journey as I went from dreams to reality, most of it very painful. I came to accept it even though life handed me many unpleasant situations. With faith and hope, however, I survived. I learned that hope is a gift that results from our faith. Hope, like faith, does not come or grow automatically. I knew from a very early age that I would have to deal with the certainties and the uncertainties of life each day. I also realized that in order to give life my best, I would have to prepare myself physically as well as mentally in order to make a meaningful contribution. To reach my goals I had to gain knowledge, character, integrity, and desire to fulfill my aims and goals. Although I was often accused of being a *métisse* (half-breed), I felt at a young age that life was going to be worth the struggle, and I was worth the effort to get the most from it.

Chapter 1

MÉTISSE

"Métisse!"

"*Tay lai*! *Tay lai*!" my schoolmates screamed as they chased me down the streets of Bien Hoa, pelting me with rocks or any other handy objects they could find. Occasionally their missiles hit their intended mark. Tears would well up in my eyes, and I would let out an involuntary groan.

I did not know what hurt more, the sharp-edged rocks or the cruel verbal jibes they hurled at me. I was determined, however, that they would never see me cry or know the true extent of my fears. Instead, I vowed to avoid them the best I could and prayed that God would deliver me from the hands of my young enemies.

By the age of six I learned skills that resembled a military strategist. Every morning I would vary the time I left home or the route I took to school, or both. It was better for me to keep my ten or fifteen tormentors off guard than to have them catch me unaware, for I knew what awaited me if they did catch me.

On those rare occasions when I allowed my thoughts to drift or my gait to slow down, the gang would seize its opportunity. Lying in wait, they would spring out and grab me as I passed by. When I tried to run away they would chase me, screaming in their shrill little voices.

"Métisse!"

"Tay lai!"

If they caught me the children would encircle me, then pinch me wherever they could as they pushed me toward a huge mango tree close to the school. This tree had an anthill next to it, and any disturbance sent platoons of determined defenders out of their fortress to attack the intruder. After grabbing my lunch, the gang would tie me from chest to foot to that mango tree, binding me with ropes and handkerchiefs that had been securely knotted together. Then they would circle the tree in a sort of ritual dance and recite in singsong fashion:

May la, tay lai!
May thich day goc xoai!
Tao phat may dong hai!

You are the half-breed!
You like to pee by the mango tree!
I fine you a dollar twenty!

All the while, the gang kept a safe distance from the angry ants, which were now crawling all over and ferociously biting me.

"Why are you doing this?" I asked, hoping for some mercy. "I have never done anything to you!"

I knew exactly why they treated me this way. I was what the French called a *métisse* (pronounced "ma TEES") and the Vietnamese, *tay lai* (pronounced "tay LIE")—a half-breed. Being half French and half Vietnamese, many of the people of my country considered me an outcast, subhuman, and therefore deserving of their contempt and vicious attacks.

However, life was not always so cruel to me. I remember my early years when I received constant love and affection from my mother and my family.

Chapter 2

The Love Story Begins

My grandfather owned Maria restaurant in Bien Hoa, Vietnam, since 1936. The business was named after my oldest aunt, whom the French soldiers had affectionately dubbed Maria. However, Aunt Maria was really named "Number Four," since her three older siblings had all died at birth.

By early 1947 the restaurant had become popular not only with the Vietnamese but also with the soldiers of the French army as well. Almost a year before, fighting broke out between the French and the Viet Minh, who sought to drive the French out of Vietnam, thus beginning the Indochina War. The Viet Minh successfully defeated the Japanese in their attempt to rule Vietnam; and after Japan surrendered to the allied forces at the end of World War II, the Viet Minh forces declared Vietnam an independent state and Ho Chi Minh its new leader. When the French tried to gain control of their colonies once again, the Viet Minh attacked.

My aunts and my mother, who was twenty years old at the time, helped in the restaurant every day. The French officers and soldiers came to enjoy the exceptionally good Vietnamese food.

In April 1947 a tall French major with brown eyes and dark, wavy hair, who appeared to be in his mid-thirties, became a regular customer for breakfast, having his favorite omelet each time. During his frequent visits he became familiar with the staff and the operation of this family-owned-and-operated restaurant and soon introduced himself to Grandfather as Major Maurice Bouttoir. As the major was having his usual breakfast one morning in May, he was delighted to discover that my mother spoke fluent French.

Like most soldiers in a foreign land thousands of miles away from home, he was lonely. To hear his native tongue spoken so impeccably well by such a beautiful young Vietnamese woman was too good to be true. Having finished his omelet, he leaned his medium frame and broad shoulders across the table toward her and looked as if he could touch every word coming from her full lips. Finally, realizing the lateness of the hour, he arose from his chair with the comment that he must get to the French compound and begged forgiveness for his hasty departure.

From that day on the major always made it a point to seek out this young beauty and engage her in conversation. As they talked he would feast his eyes on her slim, youthful figure dressed in the long, silky, white traditional Vietnamese garb, which contrasted sharply with her dark, delicate, Asian features—thick, black, shiny hair that ran halfway down her back and large, almond-shaped eyes as black as the darkest night, except for the reflection of what appeared to be a thousand lights in them, mirroring the early morning sun that poured through the restaurant window.

At first their conversations were lighthearted and of things in general, but an undercurrent began to flow between them that escaladed with each succeeding topic. Eventually their talks turned to more personal matters, especially about the owner and his family. Major Bouttoir learned that she was the seventh in a family of ten daughters and one son and that Grandfather simply called her "Number Seven." "*Co Bay*!" the major said in Vietnamese. "Miss Number Seven." The name stuck, so Co Bay she became to him from that moment on.

By June their attraction for one another had reached a level where Grandfather had begun to notice. Their desire for each other was very obvious, although they had no physical contact.

Then one morning in late June 1947, Major Bouttoir approached Grandfather and asked for his daughter's hand in marriage. He explained that he was already married with a family back in France and could not take my mother home with him when his tour of duty was over. Even though the family pleaded with Grandfather not to allow the marriage to take place, he decided it was best under the current conditions to approve the union, however short it might be. A little happiness might perhaps be better than none at all. Much more important to Grandfather was the fact that with all the violence and rapes occurring in Bien Hoa, Co Bay would be safe inside the French compound and have a good life for a while. "C'est la guerre, ma fille!" (Such is war, my daughter!) The couple was joined in holy matrimony at the Catholic church shortly thereafter.

Co Bay had honored her father, which was important in traditional Vietnamese culture. The crux of family loyalty is filial piety, which commands children to honor their father and mother and to do everything to make their parents happy and to worship their memory. This commandment provides strength, stability, and continuity to the large family group, composed of all those from the same ancestry. It is also a powerful guardian of morality, because everyone is afraid to dishonor the memory of his or her ancestors by reprehensible behavior.

The Vietnamese custom considers marriage to be more than a union of two individuals. It is a union of two families and a means of ensuring posterity. In the selection of a wife, beauty may be important, but the parents place much more emphasis on the girl's moral character, her ability to perform household tasks, and the reputation of her family. Ideally, she should be skilled in the kitchen, a good housekeeper, and adept at needlework. The wife manages the household but is expected to accede formally to the authority of her husband. The Vietnamese speak of the two obediences to which every woman must submit. She must obey her father before marriage and her husband after marriage. Few Vietnamese women openly challenge this rule.

By mid-October 1947 Co Bay had conceived. She had been so happy the past three months living in the French compound with the major, but they viewed the coming child with mixed blessings. The joy of a child was an eternal bond between them, yet it was sad to bring new life into a world filled with the uncertainties of war. The same war that brought them together would eventually end, thereby breaking them apart—maybe forever. Co Bay started talking to her baby before she was born. She wondered many times what the future would hold for her and this new life when it came.

In 1948 Mother delivered me without my father being there. He had returned to France, because his tour of duty finished. Such is war. On the day of my birth in Bien Hoa, two groups of French officials, along with the doctor, gathered around Mother and me, bringing bottles of champagne to celebrate the event. Doctor Bucheron and Monsieur Roullain had supervised my birth. I should not say I was thankful for the Indochina War; but without it, I would not exist!

"Regarde les deux faussette, c'est une belle petite fille" (Look at the two dimples), Doctor Bucheron said. "It is a beautiful little girl." They named me Yvonne M. Roullain, later to be renamed "Tay Lai" or "Métisse" by the Vietnamese. Since my father had a wife and family in France, he could not legally give me his family

When I was four Mother, enrolled me in the French school known as Ma Soeur. The school was located next door to the Catholic church where my parents had exchanged their wedding vows and I had been baptized at the age of one month. Every morning Captain Pouley took me from Bien Hoa Airbase to the school, stopping by the Tan Tan bakery to buy a *pâte chaud* for me. All the *Ma Soeur* (Vietnamese nuns) greeted me with big hugs and smiles. At school we learned French and discipline in addition to the usual subjects of math and history. The school consisted of ten classrooms with eighty to one hundred students in each room. Even with such large classes, the nuns had no trouble maintaining control. The children either respected their position in the church and community or feared the punishment they would exact on an errant child.

Each day after lunch we took a nap for two hours. When we woke up we received a piece of bread and a banana. Ma Soeur always gave me an extra banana. However, I always gave my extra bananas to a little girl for whom I felt especially sorry. Hue was one of the orphans who lived at the school. These orphans did not receive the same loving treatment as those students who had parents. Instead, they were at the mercy of the nuns, who forced them to do all sorts of menial tasks around the school to earn their keep.

Captain Pouley picked me up at five o'clock every afternoon. After returning to the base I was permitted to ride my bicycle for thirty minutes. Then I had to shower and get ready for a delicious dinner prepared by our French male maid, known as *Maroc*. Each officer had his own Maroc, a native of one of the French North African colonies, who served his French officer wherever the military sent him. Occasionally we went to the French Officers' Club for dinner. Even at the age of four, I had already observed that the officer's life held a touch of class (c'est chic). My mother always called me "ma petite pichonnette" (my little sweetheart) and dressed me in white clothing. Everything had to match, a habit I maintain even now.

I enjoyed living at the base, even though I had no small friends. I kept busy and became interested in many different things—reading, gardening, or visiting with the other French officers. After Captain Pouley picked me up from Ma Soeur School, he took me to his office and then to the flower garden next to his office. I carefully inspected each flower. One day I discovered that the gardener cut a beautiful white flower. I became very angry and cried in French, "J'ai dit au jardinier que s'il laissait les fleurs sur l'abre, elle seraient jolies et dureraient plus longtemps, que s'il les coupait, elles faneraient et mourraient." (If you leave the flowers on the tree, they will be pretty and live longer. If you cut them off, they will wilt and die.)

The sun rises and sets; the days pass. Spring bursts into vivid shades of green, followed a few months later by autumn's brilliant reds and golds. The falling leaves seem to herald other changes to warn us of other separations as well.

The time came for Captain Pouley to depart. I could never rid myself of the fear of losing someone so close. Somehow I felt this was the last of the French I would see for a long time. My father had left, so had Doctor Bucheron and Monsieur Roullain. Now Captain Pouley was leaving. Soon all the French would be gone, leaving women like my mother with children but no husbands. Their departure would deny me, the métisse—the half-breed—,and others like me part of the love and guidance all children need and deserve as they grow up and learn to get along in the world. We would like to call out "Papa!" But who can hear us or really cares what it means?

Mother and I took Captain Pouley to Saigon and then to his ship. He held me in his arms and said, "Bon courage, Yvonne.

Adieu" (Be brave, Yvonne. Farewell). I wrapped my small arms around his shoulders and held on tight for a long time. My hands had rested on those same shoulders every morning all the way from Bien Hoa Airbase to the Tan Tan bakery and then to Ma Soeur School. I missed him already, even though he had not yet left.

As Captain Pouley's departure time drew closer and closer, my fingers loosened their tight grip until finally they dropped by my sides and off his shoulders. He kissed me on my forehead and walked very fast to get aboard the ship. As the ship slipped away from the dock, he threw his last cigarette over the side into the water. I waved to him. "Bon voyage! Adieu! Adieu!" How I wished I could get his discarded cigarette and hand it back to him so I could spend just one more moment with him. I wished for just one more whiff of the French's smell in my motherland.

Mother and I now moved into my grandfather's house. Not long after that, we had to face the flood (Nuoc lut nam thin). My father tried to return once again to Indochina to save me from the flood and to take me back to France. Unfortunately, life and love are not always simple. Instead of Bien Hoa, my father was sent to Tonkin, where he was injured. Before being shipped back to France, he told Mother, "I will come back for my daughter."

In 1954 when the French left I was six years old. Suddenly I began noticing a different treatment toward me, first from Ma Soeur. All of their hugging, kissing, and doting on me left along with the French. "Très gentille petite fille" (cute little girl,) now became "métisse." Right then I grew up and began to face the cruel, real world. In that moment I felt the first scar on my emotions, but at the same time observed a special, new power flooding my mind—an inner strength that would see me through any situation that came my way.

With the French gone, Vietnam's struggle for independence became enmeshed in broader and more complicated issues of the Cold War. While the military battle was raging, steps were being taken to bring a negotiated end to the Indochina War. Ho Chi Minh let it be known that he was ready to discuss peace, and France was unable to continue the war. In February 1954 the "Big Four" meeting in Berlin agreed that a conference should be held to seek a solution for Korea and the Indochina War. Representatives of the United States, France, the United Kingdom, the Soviet Union, Communist China, Laos, Cambodia, the state of Vietnam, and the Democratic Republic of Vietnam met at Geneva in April. Two days after the opening of the conference, the Franco-Vietnamese statement was made public, declaring Vietnam to be fully independent.

At the end of May the supposedly strongly fortified position the French had established near the small mountain village of Dien Bien Phu fell after a fifty-six-day siege by the Viet Minh forces. This decisive defeat and the popular pressure in France for a rapid conclusion in the Indochina War hastened negotiations. A military truce, agreed to on July 21, partitioned the country at the seventeenth parallel. It also provided for the total evacuation of the South by the Viet Minh forces. The agreement stipulated a period of three days, during which freedom of movement was to be allowed for all persons wishing to move from one sector to the other. An International Control Commission, with representatives from India, Canada, and Poland, was formed to supervise the truce arrangements. In addition, a protocol supplementing the conference agreements scheduled free election for 1956 to reestablish the unity of the country with preliminary discussions to begin in 1955.

In May 1957 President Eisenhower and President Ngo Dinh Diem jointly reaffirmed their desire for close cooperation in working for Vietnam's freedom and independence. Their statement reiterated the American position at Geneva in 1954 that aggression or subversion threatening the political independence of South Vietnam would be considered as endangering peace and security. The conflict between North and South Vietnam intensified when they aligned themselves with opposing powers in the Cold War.

The Geneva Agreement ended the special position of French influence in Vietnam and introduced South and North Vietnam into world politics as independent entities.

President Diem refused to hold elections to reunite the two countries. His rule became increasingly dictatorial; and in 1963 a military coup overthrew and assassinated him. The South looked to the United States for aid in its development of defense, while the North formally moved into the orbit of the Soviet Union and Communist China.

Chapter 3

THE CONSEQUENCES OF BEING A MÉTISSE

With the French departure, a new chapter of our lives began. Mother withdrew me from Ma Soeur School and enrolled me in the third grade at the Vietnamese school. My teacher was Aunt Thanh (Mother's cousin). At first I had a difficult time understanding the Vietnamese language, which I had not been exposed to in the French compound. As a result, I spent two years in the third grade. Because I did not know the Vietnamese alphabet with its other characters that denoted high voice, low voice, or questions very well, the spelling on my written assignments was atrocious, thus forcing me to daily whippings at the hands of Aunt Thanh. After ordering me to lie flat on my stomach on the floor, she would take a long, thin stick and hit me across the bottom ten times, leaving red marks wherever the rod hit.

As a dutiful daughter, I had to tell Mother about my whippings before Aunt Thanh did. When I was punished in school, it embarrassed the family. I became determined, however, that I would become the best student in the class.

The second year Mother was my teacher. As the teacher's daughter, she expected me to be the best in the class; otherwise both of us would be embarrassed. In addition to labeling me "métisse" or "tay lai," the Vietnamese has accused me of being hardheaded, although I was quite intelligent. I also had to live in the discipline of the Vietnamese family culture. Not only must I please my mother, but also my grandfather, aunts, and uncles as well.

Mutually-supporting forces are brought together to train the child in Vietnam. The parents demand that the child submit to their guidance without question, argument, or hesitation. Back talk from a child is shocking to adults, and independence is discouraged. Children must always ask a parent's permission to do anything they might do and are expected to keep the parents closely informed of their activities and whereabouts. The main responsibility for the child's training and upbringing rests with the parents; but uncles, aunts, as well as older brothers and sisters, also command respect. When the child goes to school, teachers also uphold these views. Girls soon learn that their destiny lies in pleasing a husband and managing a home.

The family ancestors play an important role in the process of socialization, which the child undergoes. In the traditional Vietnamese household, the child becomes very aware of these unseen senior kinsmen. He or she comes to feel their presence and learns that they are deeply involved in his or her life. The child learns to fear, respect, and admire them from parental accounts of their strengths and virtues. Family members are thrifty, prudent, polite, peaceful, humble, conscientious, industrious, self-sacrificing, stoic, devoted, and faithful to their own parents and ancestors, and the child is urged to follow their example.

In our family we had to eat breakfast before we went to school in the morning. My favorite breakfast was Simaco (a brand name of sardines imported from France). Usually I ate a sardine sandwich, a sweet potato, a piece of papaya, and fresh carrot juice. At lunchtime, we had to wait for the oldest member of the family to come to the table first. The youngest was last. This is in keeping with the Vietnamese culture of showing respect for the elders. All the girls were expected to know how to cook, even though we had a maid.

The most important force for harmony was family loyalty. The basic social unit was the large household of an older husband and wife, their married sons, daughters-in-law, and grandchildren. While today this extended social unit is becoming less common, family ties still reach out as they have for thousands of years in Vietnam.

When I was eight my family became even stricter with me. They expected high grades from me in school. My duties included doing well in school, being respectful and polite, and learning how to become a lady.

I was permitted to go to the movies once a month, but only if the whole family went. My favorite Indian actor was Ganessang. Every picture he starred in was a story about love, courage, and sacrifice that challenged his faith. Being a hero, he always successfully met and overcame any and all challenges that came his way. My favorite movie was *An Do* or *India*. The story was excellent, and I loved the belly dancing. I would spend hours mimicking the dancers in the film. Even today I enjoy performing those dances.

Although the movie cost only five piasters (about five cents), I sometimes found myself without funds and refused to ask my family for a handout. Therefore, I had to find a way to earn the money on my own. Oftentimes I would work in Aunt Maria's restaurant. One day I noticed all the half-empty bottles of soy sauce sitting on the tables. I gathered them up, poured them all into one large bottle, and then washed the empty containers. Every afternoon an old woman would come down our street buying empty bottles. That day I sold her enough empty bottles to earn five piasters and a trip to the movies. From an early age I realized the importance of not depending on my family for everything.

The Vietnamese children at school were always waiting for me near the school entrance to steal my sardine sandwich and taunt me with this poem:

May la, tay lai!
May thich day goc xoai!
Tao phat may dong hai!

This punishment went on continually. They took my breakfast and tied me up to the mango tree for the ants to bite me. I have two large scars on my forehead from the time my schoolmates picked up a large, sharp rock and carved my forehead, because I was cute, intelligent, and had white skin. Even more disturbing is the fact that the ringleader of the group was the same little girl whom I had taken pity on at the Ma Soeur School, the one that I gave my banana to every day. Looking at her while she carved into my delicate skin, I did not hate her. The Ma Soeur treated me kindly when she was not treated kindly. She jumped at the chance to show me what the future held for a métisse. It seems to be one of life's rules that the one you help the most is often the same one who will hurt you the most.

I never told my mother what happened at school. Somehow I believed in my own strength, that I could take whatever they gave me and learn to cope with it. Each day the children delighted in tormenting me, telling me what new punishment they would exact on me the next day—splashing ink on my white clothes or making a big circle around me and taking turns pinching me, throwing rocks at me, or putting clay in my mouth.

Each morning I would run to school, varying my arrival time so I could miss as many of my tormentors as possible. I always ran straight to what I called the "little mountain," a small, mountain-like structure made from rocks with an enclosure that contained the statue of the Virgin Mary and a cross. "I can be safe here," I told myself. Since I did not know how to pray with fancy words, I just sat down next to the cross and started talking, "Chua Jesus xin bao ve con" (Lord Jesus, please protect me).

I would quietly take inventory of myself, feeling my power. I felt God was with me, so I could face whatever crisis came my way. Next, I would open my sardine sandwich, peacefully enjoying every bite of my delicious breakfast. By the time I finished, it was time to go to school. I would enter the classroom just as the bell rang. Class had already begun.

At break time I always stayed in the classroom to avoid the children and their cruel antics. I could not go to the bathroom, outside to play, or buy a snack or drink without the risk of more injuries. Each morning Mother gave me one piaster (about one cent) to buy a drink, but I always saved it. One day, some weeks earlier, I had discovered a Pilot black ink pen made in Japan in a glass case at the local shop. I had never wanted anything as much as I wanted that pen. Every time I walked by the store, I would stop and stare at the beautiful pen, which cost three hundred and twenty piasters. For three hundred and twenty days I saved my snack money, each day depositing one piaster into my piggy bank.

I never will forget the day I broke the piggy bank, pressed the money with a cast iron, put the money in an envelope, and took the money to the store to buy the pen. As soon as I got home I tried it out by signing my name on all of my schoolbooks. It was a very sophisticated signature.

The first essay I wrote with my pen was entitled "The Ice Cream Boy," followed by "A Beggar." My teacher was so impressed with my writing, she read the essay to the class. She also wrote a letter to my mother saying, "Yvonne has a very special talent for writing." When my mother and the rest of the family read my essay, they looked at me with surprise, hardly knowing what to say. Many times before I had gotten spanked for "talking like a philosopher and preaching like a Buddhist monk." Now they discovered that I could also write.

"What would you like to become when you grow up?" Mother asked me.

"A famous author," I answered.

"No," my family said all at once. "We want you to become a lawyer."

I bowed my head down to accept their decision, while trying to conceal my own decision to become a famous author.

"When you become a lawyer you can form your own opinions, but for now, if we hear any more philosophy from you, not only will you get spanked but you will also have to kneel out in the sun for two days," my aunt said.

When I heard the word *sun*, I was horrified, and I remembered what one of my spankings was for. I had to go to Grand Aunt's house every afternoon to pull gray hairs out of her head until she fell asleep. I would then walk very carefully to the big old cabinet inlaid with mother-of-pearl. I took the key from top of the cabinet. I opened it and reached for her Buddhist Bible. Next, I took the book and went out and sat under a papaya tree at the rear of the house to read it. Carefully watching the clock, I made sure that the book was back in the cabinet before my Grand Aunt woke up. It took me a few months of these stolen moments to finish reading the entire set. Grand Aunt did not want anybody to touch those books and had spanked me when she overheard what I told my cousin Jeannette.

"Our Grand Aunt gave the monk food and money for the temple, but she wouldn't give a penny to a beggar."

"I noticed that, too," remarked Jeannette almost under her breath.

"Grand Aunt believes the reason there are beggars in this life is because they had waste in their last life; therefore they should be punished for being a beggar," I declared somewhat indignantly.

"That is the way she believes."

"My philosophy is different. If you cannot give food to the beggar or share some of yours with the one that is needy, then you will put yourself in the category of the beggar in your next life. Besides, if you are a true believer, bad thoughts should never occur in your mind to wish to someone."

"Grand Aunt also believes that Buddha will take care of everything, like Buddha will give her rice. Her husband will bring the money home to pay for the maid and the utility bill. All she has to do is pray for it."

Jeannette added, "I remember every time you and I wanted to go to the movies but didn't have the money, I would pray to both Buddha and God to drop us some money from the sky. But you were the one that came up with the idea to clean all of Aunt Maria's soy sauce bottles and sell them so we could go to the movies. So I don't pray anymore."

"I would like for you to continue to pray to God. We can pray for our loved ones, health, happiness when sorrow occurs, our joys as well as anxiety, our success along with our failures. All of this contributes to one thing; it is called "faith." By that I mean when we pray we have to have faith, and faith is what we believe. When we believe strongly, we will know ourselves; and when we know ourselves, we can cope, accept, and manage our lives wisely."

"What was the other trouble that you got in with Grand Aunt? I remember I sneaked under the table to put the menthol medicine in your wound where the rod hit," Jeanette said.

"That was the day Grand Aunt came back from the temple. She said that she had prayed for all of us girls to become good. If one of us became a prostitute, she would consider that a big embarrassment that would tarnish the whole generation."

When I heard that I was upset and I said to Grand Aunt, "You cannot pray on one hand and criticize on the other hand. Besides, if you are a true believer, you should not look down on the people regardless of their race, their knowledge, their situation, what they did, or where they came from."

Grand Aunt was screaming loudly; she called for her daughter.

"You come and help me to tie this girl under the table, and I'm going to whip her for telling about my beliefs."

Grand Aunt kept asking me while she was whipping, "Are you still protecting the prostitute?"

"I am just speaking the true facts of life with my own beliefs," I said.

Grand Aunt started screaming again and said, "Now she talks about the facts of life. Whip her some more and make her kneel out in the sun for a whole day."

The reason they wanted to punish me that way was because I could not tolerate the sun. I got real bad headaches and my eyes became inflamed. They thought that by doing that I would be very miserable, therefore my thinking would change.

But my thoughts would never change, because I knew those were the correct ones.

Jeannette started crying and talking at the same time. "It hurt me so much when I had to witness all of the whippings they gave you. Why don't you forget about becoming an author and just do what the family expects you to do?"

"Becoming a famous author is the goal that I have set for my life. I'm not going to change my mind."

My schoolmates, however, were not impressed with my speaking or writing talent and continued to show me no mercy.

"Hey, Métisse," they asked, " from which hole did you crawl into the school today? Where is your father? Why don't you get out of here and go to France so you can eat butter with him?" Only the educated people ate butter at that time.

Unfortunately, they finally discovered my hiding place, my little mountain. Having sought sanctuary inside one morning, I was surprised when they broke into my little hideaway and shouted, "Hey, Métisse, you think you can get away from us by hiding in this place?"

They left me alone after that. For the first time I believed that God was so powerful and so special. He saved me once and will save me again and again throughout my life. I began to practice the complex techniques of thinking with faith, not fear. Faith is believing and fear is frightening. As a result of my new positive cast on thought, I learned to believe in myself from that day on, for I knew God was with me. I then had no fear of the shadows that had once frightened me.

I often asked Aunt Maria what my father looked like.

"Very elegant. He liked to smile. I guess he wanted to show his dimples," she explained.

"Do you think he might try to find me one day again?"

"He might. He has tried it before."

I dreamed of finding him one day. I missed the feeling of a father's love.

The maid served dinner to our family. After we ate she would eat the leftovers, which usually were only the vegetables and sauce to eat with the rice. I felt bad every time I left the dining table. Occasionally I took some fish and some meat from my bowl and hid them under the rice, acting like I was eating, but I saved them for the maid. That way at least she got to eat fish and meat once in a while.

Chapter 4

A Beautiful Bud Unbloomed

In 1963 Grandfather passed away. Aunt Maria took over the restaurant and converted it into a bar, changing Maria's into the Mekong Bar. The bar occupied the front half of the building, while our living quarters occupied the back half. None of us children were permitted to enter the bar, making us curious of all the strange, wonderful sounds we heard emanating from there.

When none of our elders were around, my cousin Jeannette, who was three years my junior, and I often stared through the large crack in the door that separated the business from the lodging. Since the split was too high, we pushed a stool over to the door and took turns spying on the bar's patrons. For the first time I saw an American kissing one of the bar girls. I felt embarrassed and excited. Although the police allowed only five girls to work in each bar at a time, Aunt Maria employed twenty. Every night when the police came to inspect the bar, most of the girls had to run and hide. I felt sorry for them and even prayed they would not get caught. Such a shame for all those pretty girls, but *c'est la guerre!* (that's war!) You do what you have to do to survive. It puts another bowl of rice on the table for the family.

The bar's owner paid them no salary. Their only income was half of the money the owner received from the drinks the customers bought for them.

One time I overheard my aunt say she was going to fire a girl simply because she was pregnant and could no longer produce the money for the bar. I felt so bad and asked myself how could my aunt do that to a pregnant woman. I realized life is full of *why*, *what*, and *because*. I went to my school notebook and took the money out of the envelope that I had saved. That night I waited for the young woman. Before she went home, I put the money in her hand and told her:

"Take care of yourself and your baby. Have faith in God and you will make it."

She looked at me, but did not have a chance to say thank you because I immediately walked away, retreating to my room so my aunt would not see me.

I was in my third year of high school. Although my schoolmates no longer chased me, I had new problems with other girls. They walked toward me and "accidentally" bumped into my chest to find out if my breasts were real or fake. Once done, they would walk away and say to the other, "She inherits from the French."

For a short while I thought I was through with the abuse. Then one afternoon a male teacher asked me to stay for a few minutes after school. While I stood next to him watching him look over my papers, he put his hand on my shoulders and forced me to the floor. I didn't know what was happening at first. As he tore off my lower clothes and then ripped his pants open, I realized what he intended to do with me. All those terrible stories I heard about rape began racing through my mind, this time with me as the victim.

Terrified, I could not breathe. I struggled to get away from him, but my slim, ninety-pound frame was no match for his strength and wicked determination. Besides, there was no one around who cared enough about me to rescue me from this vile attacker. My screams went unnoticed. Once again, the métisse received cruel, unjust treatment simply because she was a métisse. For a moment I drifted back to my early childhood when I had seen the Maroc cut the beautiful, white flower off its stem and watched as its soft, white petal wilted in the hot summer sun.

Once the teacher was through with me, he stood up and walked away as if nothing unseemly had happened. Somehow I managed to get to my feet and put my clothes on. Then I ran from the room as fast as I could and did not stop running until I reached the safety of my home. I closed the door behind me.

I felt so ashamed, but I also realized that it was not my fault. In Vietnam, the ranking Vietnamese considered it a source of pride, what Americans call "a feather in the cap," to have had a French métisse.

"What should I do?" I asked myself. "Should I tell my mother? No! I don't want my mother to hurt." Therefore I decided to muster all the strength God could give me and go on with my life, bearing this burden alone. I also knew the hurt would never completely leave me, because the teacher had taken away from me the one thing most Vietnamese girls value above all—their virginity. For many, it is the only treasure they can give to their husbands on the wedding night. What precious gift could I give to my husband?

Meanwhile, my family thought that I was not feeling well because of my monthly period. As days passed into weeks, I learned to forgive and forget this tragedy. There were so many more important things for me to do, like writing to my father in my notebooks telling him how much I needed his love.

April 1963

Cher Papa:

I've passed my geometry test today. I made several mistakes. Good thing I didn't tear the page off my notebook. I would be in big trouble with Mother, because she has marked all my pages from one to one hundred.

July 15, 1963

Cher Papa:

I am fifteen today. I probably will receive a birthday card from you if you know where to send it. I have always wished that I could send you one. I hope that maybe I will have the chance to do it one day. I always dream of you even though I don't know what you look like. I have missed your love.

Ta petite fille [Your little daughter].

Yet all the while I knew that he would never read any of my notes because I did not know who he was or where I could find him. Around that time I watched a show on television that showed an American outdoor scene, which made me dream of France and how the country and my father must look. I prayed for a magic button that I could push to bring my father and me together. I realized that God would answer that prayer one day. Until then, my pencils and paper became my best friends. With their help I poured out my innermost thoughts and deepest pains.

When I entered college in 1966, Mother quit teaching. I enrolled in VAA School (Hoi Viet My), the largest English school in Saigon, to learn English. Each day after school I walked to Mac Dinh Chi Street to catch the bus home to Bien Hoa.

In March 1967 the city of Bien Hoa was off-limits to all American servicemen for a while, because enemy rockets had shelled the airbase. All the bars were closed. As usual, after coming home from a long day at school in Saigon, I played badminton with my cousin, Jeannette. One time while we were playing outside in our backyard when we noticed an American watching us play. When I acted surprised Jeannette nonchalantly remarked that three Americans had just moved into the house next door.

"Colonel Thanh came to our house this afternoon and informed our family that he had rented his two-story house to them.

"He also told our family that he surmised that they work for either the Central Intelligence Agency or the Criminal Investigation Division of the U.S. Army."

"Jeannette, that American is still standing there and watching us," I said.

"You must be watching him, too, otherwise you wouldn't have noticed that he is watching us. Concentrate on our game."

I was embarrassed over Jeannette's statement. I also wanted to know if she knew anything else about the Americans. "Did Colonel Thanh say anything else?" I asked.

"Colonel Thanh said that if those three Americans move out, another three would move in. He consumed half the bottle of cognac by himself this afternoon."

"Our Uncle Hai didn't come today."

"No, he wasn't feeling good."

Uncle Hai was our distant uncle; he was my Grand Aunt's nephew. This uncle came to our house almost every day to drink cognac with Colonel Thanh and other friends. The only thing they drank was cognac mixed with carbonated soda. After a few drinks, they laughed and talked, mostly about politics.

The next afternoon while we played our usual game of badminton, the same American came out of his house and introduced himself to us.

"Hello, I'm Ben. What's your name?"

"I am Jeannette, and this is my cousin, Yvonne."

"May I play a game with you?" he asked.

"Yes," Jeannette replied.

Ben played with us for almost an hour. I tried not to let him know that I was looking at him. He had blonde hair with a beautiful smile and a very intelligent face. He had on beige pants and a white shirt; he looked sharp. As our eyes met I noticed his eyes were blue, and I figured him to be about six foot three inches tall.

As Ben departed, Jeannette and I looked at each other without speaking a word. That night, however, I could not sleep. Ben's face kept appearing in my mind. It made me feel good inside every time I thought about him. I could hardly wait until our next badminton game, hoping Ben would join us once again. I was shy and scared, but oh, so excited.

A few weeks and several badminton games later, Ben offered to teach us English. I told him that he would have to ask my family's permission before we could come over to his house for English lessons. Since Ben lived next door, the family consented to our visiting him from seven to nine o'clock each evening. After only two nights Jeannette stopped; I continued to see Ben.

Each night, Ben would knock on the gate at about 7:00 p.m.; the maid would call me: "Mr. Blue Eyes is knock, knock."

I was ready with my English book in my hand. I tried not to show my family that I was so anxious. They watched every move I made.

I bowed my head with respect to Mother and to my aunts. This is a Vietnamese custom that teaches children to show respect—to bow when you leave and when you return.

I walked out to the gate where Ben was standing with a pleasant smile on his face, waiting for me.

"Hi," he said.

"Hi," I said softly, but I tried not to look at him. I was so shy and nervous every time I was with him.

We walked toward his gate, just two feet away. He opened his gate and we walked upstairs to the living room.

I handed Ben the book and said, "It is called *English for Today*. This is the book they use to teach us at the VAA."

Four months later while Ben and I were spending our evening alone after the English lesson, he became very quiet and serious. Taking my hand in his, he looked into my eyes. His features appeared so stern. He acted as if he had something important to say, but said nothing and did nothing except continue to hold my hands and stare deeply into my eyes. Ben was such a gentleman.

Growing more uncomfortable by the moment, I began to feel some unknown obsession rising from within me, a sort of tidal wave of emotions. My heart began pounding in my chest and in my ears, so loud that I was certain Ben heard it too. What should I do? What could I do?

I soon realized that I was becoming frightened. The fear was creeping up slowly but surely as my face grew warm and red. My breath was coming in short gasps, and I just knew I was going to collapse. The suspense and anxiety increased to the point that I could not speak. I just sat across from Ben like a statue of Buddha and stared back into his beautiful blue eyes. Even though I was nineteen, I was extremely shy and became embarrassed at the slightest provocation.

That night, lying in my bed, sleep refused to come. I kept smelling the hands that Ben had held earlier. My thoughts of Ben persisted until time eventually led me into a deep sleep with the beautiful dreams of an innocent woman who had just fallen in love for the first time.

After that my relationship with Ben grew stronger each day.

He would stand on the balcony and wait for me to come home from school. When he saw my shadow on the dirt road turn around the corner, he would start waving, and with a smile on his face, he asked, "It must have been a long day at school. Are you ready for some more?"

I looked up at the balcony where he was standing and replied, "If the teacher is ready to teach, I'm willing to learn. It doesn't matter what page we cover tonight."

"English is a little complicated sometimes, but I think we can manage it," Ben said.

By that time I had arrived at my gate and we waved at each other again.

"I will see you at seven," Ben said. That night while we went over some of my homework from the VAA, Ben told me, "Let's take a break and get some fresh air." He then reached for my hand and helped me up from the sofa. We walked outside and stood on the balcony. Ben pointed his left hand up to the sky and said, "It's almost a full moon tonight."

I looked up where he was pointing, and I noticed he had rested his right hand on my shoulder. I began to get excited. I felt Ben was squeezing me and pulling me closer to him. I tried harder to control myself, but my heart began pounding very fast in my chest. I didn't realize that my head was touching Ben's arm. I felt good as I wondered what was going to happen next; my hands still rested on the balcony railing, and I noticed they were cold. Ben turned his head down and tried to touch his head to mine.

"What are you thinking so hard about?" Ben asked.

I turned my head and looked at him; as our eyes met, our faces were closer. I spoke falteringly and seemed scarcely conscious of what I said. I heard no words, only the soft voice, more familiar to me than my own. I didn't want to open my eyes. I was afraid the good feeling might disappear. Ben had filled me with frenzied intoxication for the first time. We were still in each other's arms and kissing. The moon was bright enough to witness us, with a love song in our hearts, disregarding the jealousy of the moon.

I was so very happy, yet so sad, because I knew that Ben would one day depart from me.

On September 10, 1967, a man who worked at the Catholic church in Bien Hoa appeared at our house. "Is this the place that used to be Maria's restaurant?" he asked.

"Yes," my aunt replied.

The man handed a letter to my aunt and left. She looked at the envelope and said, "It's for you, Yvonne," then handed it over to my mother to open. The return address read: Pere Dozande, Nguyen Du Street, Saigon. Mother carefully opened the letter and read it aloud to everyone.

> Chère Mademoiselle Yvonne, I have received a letter from your father from Saint Genis Pouilly, France. He would like for me to locate a child by the name of Yvonne Roullain. She was born July 15, 1948, in Bien Hoa and was baptized at the church in Bien Hoa when she was one month old. The last known address where she might be after the French left was Maria's restaurant in Bien Hoa. The restaurant was owned by her grandfather, who was well known. Please come down to Nguyen Du Street, Saigon, to see me so you can get your father's address. He is waiting to hear from you.

My family was shocked. All speaking in unison, "Your father has kept his promise!" they proclaimed. Who would think after all these years that this Frenchman was still looking to find his daughter?

"Yvonne, you are very lucky. You must have been good to God," my aunt spoke quietly. I was sitting at the dining table and wondering if I was dreaming. I swear I saw hundreds of angels in heaven singing. I wanted to shout, "Merci, mon Dieu!" (Thank you, my God!). But my tongue was tied in a big knot. My faith had reached to heaven. "God loves me and He is always with me," I assured myself.

I tried to visualize what my father looked like now and how soon I would meet him. Dinner was served, but I could not eat. I was already full—full of happiness, dreams, and hopes that tomorrow would change my life forever.

The next morning, Mother, my aunt, and I traveled to Saigon to meet with Père Dozande. He handed us a letter my father had sent him, pointing to my father's address on the envelope. Père Dozande's eyes were full of tears, and so were mine. "Write to your father," he said.

As soon as we got back home, I started writing a letter to my father. There were so many things I wanted to say, yet I did not know what to say or how to begin. The shock that I might soon be reunited with my father was beginning to set in. My most ardent dream might actually become a reality. For the first time in my life, I felt that I really had a father. I poured out all my good feeling to him and hoped that I would hear from him very soon. I mailed the letter the next morning.

> Dear Papa:
>
> This is the first time in my life that I have actually written to you. I wrote to you in the past, but only on my student notebooks. I have called out, "Papa," many times in my dreams, and I have imagined your portrait. I have missed your love and have prayed for our reunion one day. I hope that this letter will be the bridge to bring us together. My best wishes to you.
>
> Your little daughter,
>
> Yvonne

Next time I saw Ben, I told him all about my father.

"I have found my father," I said.

Ben looked at me for a few seconds and said, "I'm very happy for you. I know how much it means to you."

"It's not a dream anymore! It's a reality!" I shouted in my little voice.

Ben reached out and held me tight in his arms. He wanted to share some of my happiness, which I never had before and was experiencing at this moment.

September proved to be an exceptionally good month.

On October 10, 1967, one of my worst fears came true. Ben held my hands and said, "No English lesson tonight; I am leaving on October 31."

"Huh," was the only word I said. I was flabbergasted and shocked.

Ben appeared to be sad; he didn't talk much. After a few moments, we tried to comfort our grief by kissing each other. We never had kissed so much as that night.

"Only twenty more days for us to spend together," Ben said.

I nodded my head and agreed.

"I would like for you to have dinner with me tomorrow. I will come and ask your family's permission."

"I hope that they will agree."

That night, Ben had ordered food from La Plage, one of the famous restaurants in Bien Hoa. He had set a little table with two chairs in the living room where we spent every night for my English lessons. He pulled the chair on the right hand side and asked me to sit; as he sat himself across from me, he poured the orange juice for us and made a toast.

"To our first dinner together," he said.

"To our relationship," I said.

Ben reached out for a little black box, which was on the table. He opened the box and showed it to me.

"I bought this sapphire ring for you when I was on temporary duty in Bangkok. I wanted to wait for a special moment like this to give it to you."

"Thank you for thinking of me."

"There will not be any more English lessons after tonight. The only time will be for the two of us," Ben said.

Ben then pulled out a picture from his billfold and gave it to me.

"I had my Vietnamese interpreter take my picture in front of this house for you to keep to remember me when I am gone."

I held the picture in my hand like I was holding something precious. I noticed Ben's handwriting on the back of the picture:

> To Baby Yvonne:
>
> A wonderful friendship is to hold and to cherish always. Let it be so with ours.
>
> Love,
>
> Ben

I tried to control myself all of that time. My emotions were overwhelming. My tears were rolling down my cheeks faster than I could wipe them off. I looked at Ben's picture once again. I already missed him even though he was still sitting there in front of me.

Ben got up and came toward me. He wiped my tears off with his handkerchief and told me, "Yvonne, I love you. There is no human voice to describe the unutterable fervor of my love for you."

We held each other for a long time. We didn't eat the food we had ordered.

We finally exchanged our goodnight kisses. Ben walked with

me to the gate. We kissed once again before I walked into my house.

Each day seemed to get shorter and more difficult for me. I told Ben that the VAA school gave scholarships to deserving students to go to school in the United States. Perhaps I would come to America and find him. "Could love be that simple?" I wondered. Then, we were together, but in the next days we would separate to live half a world apart. Every night I cried myself to sleep. How could I endure life without Ben? No matter how bad I felt, however, I still had the responsibility to myself and to my family to maintain good grades in school.

The week before Ben left, he asked my family's permission to take me to the zoo in Saigon for the day. They gave their permission, but ordered me to be home by 5:00 p.m. It was the first time, and probably the last time, that Ben and I would spend an entire day together. I was so thankful to my family for giving us this time together.

Ben took a lot of pictures of me at the zoo. I had worn the *Ao Dai*, the traditional Vietnamese clothes, as Ben had requested.

"I am going to send you a copy of the pictures," Ben said.

"Thank you," I replied.

Although Ben was still with me, I already missed him and felt extremely lonesome. After lunch we returned home. The day passed too quickly.

On October 31 our maid came to my room and announced, "Mr. Blue Eyes wants to see you."

I ran out of the house to the gate. I opened the gate and we both stared at each other for a long time without uttering a sound.

"Time to say good-bye," Ben said.

"Have a safe trip, Ben."

I gave him two pairs of chopsticks to remember me by and declared, "I will always cherish our memories. I love you."

Ben held the two pairs of chopsticks in his hand and said, "I will look at the chopsticks once in a while to remember that we didn't have the chance to start our dinner together." He then handed me a little note.

"This is my address. Please write when you have the time."

"I will, I will," I kept repeating to myself while Ben got in the passenger seat in the Jeep. Ray, his boss, was waiting to take Ben to the airport. It was the last time my gate was knocked on at 7:00 p.m. by "Mr. Blue Eyes."

I wrapped my *English for Today* book with Ben's picture in it on October 31, 1967, and have kept them ever since.

Ben took part of my soul with him when he left Vietnam. I ached all over, but I kept telling myself there was nothing I could do about it. I yearned for him every time I passed the house next door where he lived. It was fate, I thought, and I should not feel bad. Flowers blossom only once, then wilt and die, but the heart may blossom again and again. For a moment I remembered my mother and the tragic song I heard her sing all my life. Was I singing that same song now?

> J'attendrai, le jour et la nuit!
> J'attendrai, toujour ton retour.
> I am waiting, day and night.
> I am waiting, every day for your return.

The Tet Offensive of 1968 swept the length of South Vietnam. Long Binh, Bien Hoa Airbase, Saigon, and many of the provinces were hit hard by the Viet Cong. The Viet Cong even occupied the Vinatexco Textile Mill directly across Highway One from the sprawling Tan Son Nhut Airbase and also seized Saigon's national broadcasting station. Meanwhile, Bien Hoa Airbase received numerous rockets, followed by a mortar barrage and supported ground attack with heavy machine guns. Several of the homes and businesses were destroyed, damaged, or on fire, including parts of our house. We lived six miles from the Bien Hoa Airbase.

Mother and I, along with my aunts and cousins, were in Saigon at that time to celebrate Tet, the Vietnamese New Year. We stayed with Aunt "Number Ten" in Saigon; but when the Viet Cong attacks became too close, we were evacuated to the Catholic church. When we arrived we found that dozens of people were already there. The church staff gave us bread, soybean cakes, and some rice to eat during our stay. On the first day when I received my daily ration, I noticed an emaciated, middle-aged woman with four small children standing off in the shadows. All the children, age one through five, had dirty faces and runny noses. The youngest child she held to her bosom, while the others stayed close, holding on tightly to her silky slacks. Feeling sorry for them, I handed the mother my portion, thinking they all needed it more than I did. For ten days we remained there before conditions improved enough for us to safely take the bus back to Bien Hoa.

I soon discovered there are people who supposedly extend a kind hand in aid, while actually awaiting an opportunity to take advantage of unfortunates who come their way.

Jeannette pointed her finger in the direction where the nuns were standing.

"The nuns are still busy passing out the straw mats. I wish she could find another corner for us," Jeannette said.

I looked in the direction she pointed and said, "They did what they could. We should be grateful." I noticed there was a man looking in our direction once in a while.

Being the only métisse stranded in the church, I somehow

became caught in the "tiger's eyes" of the priest. With so many seeking shelter, the church did not have enough straw mats for everyone to sleep on. They gave what they had to the elderly and small children. Therefore, all my family and several others slept on the cold, damp cement floor.

As I sat on the floor, one of the nuns approached me and explained:

"Hello, I'm Sister Loan. How many people are in your family?" she asked.

"There are eight of us," I replied.

"Father Thinh would like to see you in his office to arrange a better place for you and your family."

"Thank you, Sister." I followed her up to the priest's office. The nun opened the door, introduced me to the priest, and excused herself and left. As is our custom, I bent my head down with respect. "Da thua Cha," I said (Good afternoon, Father). No reply. I lifted my head, questioningly, and looked directly into the eyes of the young, handsome priest. Those eyes held me firmly in their grasp. Those eyes were not warm or kind. They were cold and calculating—the devil's eyes.

The young, handsome priest continued to stare at me, never blinking. He reached out and grabbed me, squeezing me tightly as he pulled me to him. Lust and desire consumed him, and rape quickly followed. Afterwards I felt very strange. Had he violated me out of human desire or because I was a métisse? I forced myself to look at him, but I could not see him clearly. Tears welled up in my eyes. I cried not only for myself, but also for him. He had a weak spirit. He was not a true man of God. For the first time I believed the world was a veil of tears and only our Creator could wipe them away.

Once we got back to Bien Hoa, the city remained off limits to all American servicemen, and the bars remained closed for several weeks. As a result, my family, which consisted of twelve relatives plus two maids, had no income.

I told my family, "I could withdraw from both college and the VAA and find work to take care of you."

"No, you don't withdraw from school," my aunt said.

"The bills need to be paid, my little cousins need food, and the maids need to get paid. Aunty, please let me work and help the family."

The family firmly rejected the offer. "We want you to finish college and three years of VAA, even though we will have to sacrifice," my aunt said.

I continued to write often to both my father and Ben during the Tet Offensive. However, I never revealed anything about our personal problems and tragedies. Instead, I dreamed of one day visiting my father in France and Ben in the United States.

Chapter 5

In the Danger Zone

When I was studying one afternoon, Kim arrived at our door on an errand for her mother, inviting Mother and my aunt to play Chinese cards with her at her home. It had been a long time since I had last seen Kim. We had been roommates in high school. After catching up on the news about each other and our families, I confided in Kim that I had been thinking about quitting school and going to work. Kim told me about an opening at the United States Agency for International Development (USAID), a branch of the United States State Department. I was excited at the news and told Kim I would contact her as soon as I could get my family's permission. They agreed, and two days later Kim and I walked into the office at USAID headquarters. Kim introduced me to the personnel officer, who gave me both a written and typing test. I passed the tests and was assigned to work in the logistics office the same day.

I was shy and nervous. My boss, Mr. Dameron, greeted me with a smile and attempted to ease my noticeable discomfort. Mr. Dameron explained that I would be working in another office with Mr. Combs when he returned from his home leave.

"When is Mr. Combs supposed to come back, sir?" I asked.

"In two weeks," Mr. Dameron replied. "In the meantime, you can look through these papers."

"Yes, sir."

Two weeks later, on July 18, 1968, Mr. Dameron brought a well-dressed man wearing a blue suit up to my desk and introduced him to me.

"Yvonne, this is Mr. Charlie Combs, your new boss."

"I am pleased to meet you, sir," I said, smiling at him.

"I'm glad to meet you too, Yvonne; and I can sure use your help. We'll be going to our office in a minute. It is just three miles from here in another compound."

I thanked Mr. Dameron for his kindness and help. "Goodbye." I waved, walked out the door with Mr. Combs, and jumped into the Scout beside him. We spent the rest of the day in our new office discussing my job as interpreter, translator, and secretary for the Region III Corps Tactical Zone.

Mr. Combs was the principal advisor and assistant to the senior logistics advisor of the Region III Tactical Zone, responsible for eleven provinces in his zone. In addition to the Vietnam Province Chiefs' staff, there were several advisors assigned to each of the provinces.

"What do you think about the job?" Mr. Combs asked after explaining all my responsibilities.

I was never afraid of the danger, but I had to think about my mother. If something should happen to me, who would take care of her? I blinked a couple of times, just long enough to communicate with God. I sincerely believed that God would not let me die before I had a chance to see my father. I also believed that God in His infinite wisdom had placed me on this earth for a purpose, which I would fulfill later in my life.

"Yes, sir. I will take this job."

"Your courage really impresses me, Yvonne. I interviewed

several men and women for your job, but they were afraid to travel under such hazardous conditions," Mr. Combs said. "The first thing I would like for you to learn is the military phonetic alphabet. For instance, instead of saying 'Viet Cong attack,' you would say 'Victor Charlie attack.'"

"Yes, sir. I understand. I will be happy to learn it."

"All right," he replied. "I am going to the maintenance shop. If I don't get back here before 6:00 p.m., go ahead and lock up the office when you leave."

Before I started working on the alphabet, however, I rearranged my desk to suit me. I believed in doing all I could to help me like my work because the office would become my second home.

That night I reported all the details of my first day at the office to my family. They asked me if my boss was nice. To which I replied, "Yes, so far."

"What about your salary?"

"My boss had to send my job requisition to the personnel office. I will probably know in a couple of days."

"Do you like your work?" Mother asked.

"Yes, Mom, I do." I did not want my mother to know just how dangerous my job was, nor the fact that I was concerned about her and what would happen to her if I should be killed by the Viet Cong. Trying to avoid further questions about my work, I politely excused myself to shower and get ready for dinner.

After dinner, I always took a walk around our backyard and looked for a flower in bloom. I plucked one flower and one Vietnamese plum and then went to sit under the papaya tree to offer to God. Since all of my family are Buddhist, the papaya tree is the only place I can pray.

I kneeled down with my eyes closed and my hands raised in prayer to the Lord.

Heavenly Father, as my day comes to a close, I bow my head in a prayer of true thanksgiving to You for this secret place to praise You. I thank You for the strength of the day. I thank You, Lord, for protecting me from all harm. Thank You, Lord, for directing me in my life and granting me wisdom to overcome all the problems and face temptation. I thank You, Lord, for blessing our family with our daily food. May You bless the poor and unfortunate for all that they need. May You heal all the sick and comfort those in sorrow. And Lord, may You bless us a good night's sleep without worrying about the rocket attack on Bien Hoa Airbase. In Jesus' name. Amen.

After I finished praying I went to the desk in my bedroom to write to Ben. While my soul yearned to say thousands of heartfelt things to him, I was perplexed, because I could not express my feelings to him.

"Writing a letter to Mr. Blue Eyes?" Jeannette looked up from her book. "Now is the perfect time for you to read this book, Yvonne. The novel is *Yeu* (Love) by Chu Tu."

I made no reply; I just watched her as she sat at her own desk across the room from mine. Her eager eyes were devouring the last page of the book. Moments later when she closed the book and looked up, I asked, "Did you finish reading *Nu Ba Vuong*?" *Nu Ba Vuong* was a book that I had loaned her several days before about an errant knight.

"Oh, yes," the dreamy-eyed girl replied. "It was great."

Jeannette and I were both avid readers. I especially liked Vietnamese and Chinese literature, as well as the works of Victor Hugo, the most famous and influential writer of nineteenth-century French literature. In addition, I read the entire set of Buddhism, which belonged to my grand aunt who was a devout Buddhist.

"I'm going to bed, Yvonne. Good night," Jeannette said sleepily.

"Good night, Jeannette." I was still sitting at my desk trying to finish a letter to Ben.

The next morning I jumped out of bed earlier than usual and got ready for work. Aunt Maria had a sardine sandwich waiting for me, which I took with me to eat for lunch at the office. I ate a breakfast of pork brain omelet with my carrot juice and papaya to sustain me on my four-mile trek to the office. Although my family urged me to buy a bicycle, I refused. I enjoyed the long walk.

When I reached the office, Mr. Combs was already there.

"Good morning, Yvonne."

"Good morning, sir."

"Will you make a pot of coffee?" he asked.

I answered, "Sir, it is not a secretary's job to make coffee."

Mr. Combs just removed his glasses and looked at me rather strangely but didn't say anything. After that the day proceeded slowly and monotonously. Neither of us talked. Hours later Mr. Combs left and shut the door behind him hard. I felt as if he had slammed the door in my face.

Upset by his behavior, I decided to await his return and tell him that I did not appreciate his theatrical departure. At four o'clock Mr. Combs returned carrying a paper bag. He walked over to my desk, opened the drawer, and placed a can of candy, a package of Fig Newtons, and a bottle of vitamins in it. After slamming the drawer shut, he reached into the bag again, this time pulling a small book, which he handed to me.

"Read this when you have time," he said. Then he walked out the door.

"Thank you, sir," I said to his back. "And would you please not cost the government another door?" He looked at me as if to say, "Who do you think you are?" but he shut the door softly as he exited.

I looked down at the book in my hand. *Secretary's Handbook.* For the next two hours I browsed through it. I had to laugh when I discovered that the book stated that one of the secretary's many duties included making coffee, but not necessarily in certain offices.

That evening I walked home with many thoughts in my mind. I had not intended to be rude to my boss, nor would I have minded fixing a pot of coffee for him. I just didn't want anyone insisting that I do something that was not listed in my job description.

As soon as I got to the office the next morning, I made a pot of coffee and anxiously awaited Mr. Combs's arrival.

"Good morning," he said as he walked in the door, a broad smile appearing across his face. "I could smell the coffee from outside. Will you please pour me a cup?"

Without reply, I poured him a cup and walked over and placed it on his desk. "I am doing you a favor, sir, because it didn't say in the handbook that I had to *pour* the coffee." Mr. Combs just smiled and nodded, apparently happy at my response.

Later that afternoon before he left the office, Mr. Combs asked me to answer the phone.

"Sir? There is no phone in this office."

"That's right."

"So, why are you doing this?"

"I have had a few dumb secretaries before. Everything I told them to do, they would say, 'Yes, sir,' without question just to please me."

"I see," I said.

"I want to give you the money to have an extra key made for this office. Would you like for me to give you a lift home?"

"Thank you, sir."

As soon as I walked in the door, my family bombarded me with questions about my second day at work. "Who brought you home?" someone asked. I politely answered their endless list of questions and then quickly excused myself for my evening shower before they could catch their breaths to ask even more questions. When I was finished and was dressed again, I asked permission to go to the market to have a key made for the office.

"Yes," Mother said, "but Jeannette must go with you, and both of you must come right back."

When I reached the office for my third day of work, Mr. Combs's vehicle was already parked outside. I wondered why he had come so early today. The heavenly smell of coffee hit me as soon as I opened the door. "How I would love a cup right now," I thought.

"Good morning, Yvonne. Would you like a cup of coffee?"

"Yes, with cream and sugar please," I answered, trying not to appear too anxious.

"Wait just a minute," Mr. Combs said, teasingly. "It doesn't say in the *Secretary's Handbook* that the boss has to make coffee for the secretary does it?"

"No," I cautiously replied.

"And it doesn't say that the boss could choose not to fix the secretary a cup of coffee with cream and sugar if he wishes?"

We looked at each other and laughed, knowing that yesterday's disagreement was amicably resolved. When we settled down to another day of work, I handed Mr. Combs the key I had duplicated. He tried the door, but it did not work. Angrily, he tossed the key in the trash can.

"Mr. Combs, I am very sorry that the key doesn't work, but you don't have to get so mad and throw it so hard in the trash can. It is the same as if you threw it in my face."

"Well, that is the way I am," he replied. "So you may as well learn to get used to my temper."

I looked straight at him. "Sir, I have had to put up with a lot of unpleasant things in my life, but there are some things I am not willing to do. I am going to the headquarters and asking permission to resign."

"I'll take you up there myself," Mr. Combs said.

"I am ready, sir."

We got in his Scout and started for the personnel office. When we arrived at headquarters, Mr. Combs asked, "Would you please come with me for a few minutes?"

I did not know what was happening, but followed him anyway. When we got upstairs, he opened the door for me. "Please sit down. I'd like to talk to you."

I looked around and did what he asked. I realized then that we were in the snack bar. "Mr. Combs, why are we here? We are supposed to be in the personnel office."

"I am very sorry. I promise that I will never lose my temper with you again. You have passed all the tests. Besides, we had to come up here to check on your salary."

Then I remembered that he really did have to check on my salary, and it was obvious by his apology that Mr. Combs did not intend to let me resign. "What would you like to do, Mr. Combs?"

"Let's have some lunch and then we'll go to personnel and return to our office."

I simply lowered my head and said nothing.

I was pleasantly surprised to discover that my salary was twelve thousand piasters per month, almost the salary of a Vietnamese major. Since I needed only three hundred piasters each month in case of any emergency, my family got the biggest portion of my income for household expenses. I did not go out for breakfast, lunch, or dinner with my friends at the office, nor did I drink or smoke. I walked the eight miles to and from work every day, so I needed no money for transportation. The three hundred piasters I had kept was more than enough to keep me supplied in black-ink Pilot pens.

Time passed, and Mr. Combs and I settled into a comfortable routine. I also continued to write Ben regularly. Since Ben's birthday was in August, I bought a tie and a few other Vietnamese souvenirs to send him. I showed them to Mr. Combs and explained that these were a birthday gift for my sweetheart, Ben. He thought that it was very nice of me to remember Ben so long after he had returned home to the United States. He even offered to mail my package through the post office at the base, so that I would not have to worry that it might get lost through the Vietnamese post office.

Mr. Combs and I had begun to travel twice a week by air to the provinces that were his responsibility. Many times the plane arrived late to pick us up. At those times, I was concerned that my mother might be worried about me. But I always believed that God was with me, protecting me from all harm. He would not let anything happen to me before giving me a chance to see my father. I also had to fulfill my responsibilities to Mother, to provide the care she needed.

To maintain this daily contact with the provinces, we used Air America, the only airline in the region. Somehow Air America always did a superior job, even under the most difficult conditions. On one of our numerous routine trips, the pilot was warned of a firefight in progress near the landing strip.

"You're a very brave man to attempt a landing under such bad condition," Mr. Combs told the pilot after hearing the report on his headset in the plane's cabin.

"No, I'm not brave," he said, smiling at us. "I'll be taking off as soon as I drop you off! You are the brave one, because you will have to stay there until I pick you up in about four hours."

The next week we returned to this province for a follow-up visit. Upon disembarking from the plane, we noticed twelve Viet Cong bodies lying on the ground. They had been killed in the battle the week before and laid out as a display to all who walked by.

Captain Boyd, who flew us frequently, always had a good joke, especially when the situation became tense. The one that Charlie and I really enjoyed was about the three insurance salesmen that were arguing the merits of their life insurance policies. The first salesman proudly stated that his company insured from the basket to the casket. The second salesman stated loudly that his company insured from the womb to the tomb. The third salesman proclaimed that he had them both beat by insuring from conception to the resurrection. Charlie once asked the pilot what actions we should take in an emergency, and his reply was, "Repeat slowly after me, 'Our Father who art in heaven...'"

Most of our pilots were ex-military officers, and their sense of humor helped us survive many hazardous situations as we flew from one province or conference to another. Mr. Combs attempted to schedule a visit to each province at least once a month to maintain continuity and to better oversee the many programs for which our office was responsible. Monsoon rains, enemy activity, and lack of available aircraft routinely disrupted his schedule. Seven of the eleven provinces we visited by air were Binh Tuy, Long An, Phuoc Tuy, Binh Long, Phuoc Long, Hau Nghia, and Tay Ninh. The other four provinces were Bien Hoa, Gia Dinh, Long Khanh, and Binh Duong. We traveled by road, which was always in the danger zone.

On November 12 Mr. Combs went to Binh Duong Province alone. At six o'clock that evening he had not yet returned. I wondered why. I did not close the office and go home as I usually did each night at this time, but knew the family might worry if I was late. Six-twenty came, but still no sign of Mr. Combs. Nervous, I began pacing the floor. I could not leave until he returned. Finally, at 6:40 he stomped into the office and slammed the door behind him.

"Charlie, I'm so happy to see you," I said.

He looked at me for a long time then crossed the room to where I was standing. He reached for my hands and held them. "Why haven't you gone home yet?"

"I'm still here because I was concerned about you and your safety."

"I appreciate that. Now, let me take you home before you get into trouble for being late."

As he drove me home, Charlie admitted that he liked me calling him by his first name. "From now on, please call me 'Charlie' and permit me to drive you to and from the office."

"Thank you for the offer," I said, "but I will have to ask my family's permission first."

"All right. Let me know tomorrow. Good night, Yvonne."

"Good night, Charlie."

After several months I came to understand Charlie much better. We communicated extremely well with each other, and I began to feel more and more comfortable around him. As I continued to work closely with him from time to time, we usually had a discussion about the world's problems and trying to solve every one of them—education, ecology, and world population. We were in tune about almost every subject we discussed.

"What is your opinion of education?" Charlie asked.

"I treat education like a challenge," I told Charlie.

"What do you mean by that?" he asked.

"By that I mean that many countries are moving into the

technological revolution. The people must be much better educated and in different ways. For instance, the high school should allow students the choice of preparing for college or using their final two years to learn electronics, computer programming, interactive graphics, or something of value that will serve them in the real world of work."

"What you are saying is the people will have a better job if they achieve a reasonable degree?" he asked.

"Yes, in this respect the challenges of education are far more complex now than they were before. Somehow, children must acquire knowledge more efficiently, especially related to skills and attitudes."

"Do you think a person can get too much education?" he asked.

"I just don't see how a person can get too much education. If anything, there's just never enough to allow us to learn to our maximum ability. I say full steam ahead with education for everyone, according to his or her own ability. You know the popular slogan 'A mind is a terrible thing to waste.' And the brain needs balanced nutrition in order to function properly!"

"You have lived in Vietnam, and you probably have read about China. What did you observe as far as population control?"

"In my opinion population control is essential to saving us all in the not-too-distant future. Our fragile earth was never intended to support an unlimited population. For the first billion years, hardly anyone considered the relationship between man and Earth's resources a problem. But for the past two thousand years, it has rapidly accelerated to what is now becoming, with each passing day, an acute problem. And recycling is only a short-term 'cure.'"

"So are the solutions simple?"

"No!"

"Are they in the not-too-distant future?"

"No!"

"What can we, as individuals, do?"

"Birth control education is throughout the rest of the world. Illegitimate childbirth has become widespread, further adding to social problems, as well as ecological concerns. Those of us who know should talk to those who don't know. Word of mouth promotes more 'sales,' so to speak, than any other form of advertising. It can be done on an much grander scale by incorporating this type of education into all school systems and by television programming."

"Too many people today simply just don't know and are unwilling to learn," Charlie commented.

"Some are unable to learn," I added.

"What do you think of life overall?"

"I'm willing to give up some of the things in order for quality of life rather than quantity of life."

"Are you willing to give up your affluence?"

"Yes, substantially! I have already 'borrowed' myself past the brink!"

"There is enough stress in the world today. Do you agree?"

"Yes, and I cannot conceive of any part of the above kind of life being stress free."

"I'm very impressed by your view of life and the wisdom within you."

"Thank you, and I use every minute of it."

"You must read a lot of books."

"A few!" I replied.

"I would like to hear more of your views on different subjects next time."

I gave him a smile. "You don't know it, but my family frequently spanked me when I was eight. They said that I talked like a philosopher and preached like a Buddhist monk."

Charlie laughed and said, "You must talk a lot."

"Only when I need to," I replied.

As time went by the danger seemed to draw Charlie and me closer together. We shared lunch together on each field trip. We began to exchange life stories and care for each other's feelings. It seemed like we were preparing for a new chapter in our lives.

On February 17, 1969, Charlie suggested that I go visit my father in France. He would arrange for me to take an extended leave from my job.

Although seeing my father had always been my greatest wish, it was impossible for me right then because I had not saved enough money.

Our relationship continued to strengthen. On weekends Charlie often invited me to go bowling with him in Saigon or occasionally to a party given by USAID Headquarters. My family, however, seldom granted permission, even though I was twenty-one years old. Many times I wished the office remained open on weekends so I could see Charlie every day. Mostly, though, I stayed home reading books, writing to my father, or teaching the maid how to read.

In April 1969 Charlie told me he would like to send me to France to visit my father, paying for the trip himself. I explained to him that I appreciated his generosity very much, and I would consider his offer.

"I love you, Yvonne. I want to see you happy. You deserve it, and you may never get this chance again. We may both get killed tomorrow or tonight while we're sleeping."

What could I say? I tried to hide my feelings for Charlie, but deep down inside I knew that I loved him. My heart began to throb for this kind, generous man. I could not share my feelings with my family. I had no friends. My upbringing had been very strict. My family taught me about loyalty, respect, moral values, principles, and to honor my parents and revere my ancestors. Filial piety was still the most respected value in Vietnamese life, manifested by veneration for departed ancestors.

Days went by. I finally wrote my father to let him know that I would like to visit him. I decided to accept Charlie's generous offer, but when Father received my letter he was so happy that he offered to pay for my airplane ticket from Vietnam to France.

My family was very excited about my trip. Since I had never in my whole life been anywhere by myself, I was overwhelmed that France, a country thousands of miles away, would be my first long journey alone. Charlie got everything in order for me—suitcases, clothes, and the airline ticket. Together we went to the French Embassy in Saigon to pick up my passport. After that, we went to the International House restaurant, which was reserved for the diplomatic corps.

As we sat at our table enjoying the food, the ambience, and each other's company, Charlie softly spoke. "I would like to tell you about my life before you leave for France. At least you will know, just in case I should never see you again."

Charlie took a sip of his coffee then gently placed the cup down in its saucer again before continuing in his low voice. "My parents were divorced when I was two years old. I do not know what happened to my father, and my mother could not keep me, so I ended up in a series of foster homes. I became an orphan at the age of two. I was sent to Father Flanagan's home, Boys Town now, on the outskirts of Omaha, Nebraska.

"I spent the next five years at this home. When I was five my Indian grandmother came to get me to live with her on her farm in Oklahoma. My grandmother died about a year later, and I was sent to a foster home. This home became unbearable after about six months of verbal and physical abuse in addition to jealousy from their own children. I ran away from this home and began a hand-to-mouth existence for several years. Begging for food during the Depression years and sleeping in a cardboard box became a way of life until I was thirteen years old. At this time the government created a program called the CCCs. This program was for boys like me and boys of poor families who could earn money to help their parents. I was taught how to operate a bulldozer tractor and spent the next three years clearing fire lanes in a national forest in Nebraska. After serving my three years tour, I was discharged. In February 1940 I joined the marines, and after completing basic training at the Marine base in San Diego, I received orders to report to the marine detachment on the island of Guam. Ten months later, after the bombing of Pearl Harbor, the United States declared war on Japan. On December 10, 1941, the Imperial Japanese Marines landed on Guam. I was taken prisoner and spent the next forty-five months in various prisoner-of-war camps in Japan.

"Since our POW camps were not marked in accordance with the Geneva Convention rules, we were subjected to hell on earth every time our own B-29 bombers came to bomb us. We received a total of five hundred raids during those months of captivity. The Japanese beat, starved, and tortured us, and the United States Air Force dropped many bombs on us. The limits of human endurance were not only tested to the limit time and time again but also might even be considered unbelievable to anyone who did not experience all this.

"When the Japanese troop ship transported us to Japan, we were packed below deck like sardines with only enough room to sit. Any movement was just about impossible. Unfortunately, most of the men became sick with diarrhea. The stench became intolerable in a very short time.

"Imagine thirst so terrible that we had to drink our own urine. Hunger forced us to eat live lizards and grasshoppers to survive.

Forced labor at the point of a bayonet consisted of carrying two-hundred-pound bags of rice on our backs up a wooden ramp from the dock to the hold of a cargo ship which was forty feet higher than the dock. This feat was accomplished by POWs that weighed less than half of the load on their back. Any slow movement or stoppage resulted in a jab from a very sharp bayonet. As POWs we received no medical care and minimal nourishment. Once a day our captors gave us watery soup and bug-infested rice. Because of this inhumane treatment, only a small number of us survived.

"On September 5, 1945, the United States Marines arrived at our camp. It was liberation day! Twenty-one of my marine buddies and I were medically evacuated to a hospital ship anchored in Tokyo Bay. From there we were flown the next day to the U.S. Naval Hospital at Great Lakes, Illinois. I spent the next twelve months in the hospital; I was twenty-four years old and weighed sixty-three pounds.

"After I was discharged from the hospital, since I was an orphan I had no home or family to go to, so one of my marine friends that was a POW with me invited me to come home with him and meet his family. He had a big family and treated me like I was one of their own.

"I stayed with my friend for about six months and then decided to go back in the service. I joined the army in 1947. This decision was based on future medical problems that may occur and were service connected. I was in Japan when the atom bombs were dropped, and I imagine that I might have gotten some radiation at that time."

Charlie took another sip of coffee and fixed his eyes on the table in front of him. He remained quiet for a long time. I continued to look at him and noticed an occasional sudden grimace crossing his face, as if he had been transported back in time and was reliving the whole torturous experience all over again.

My heart ached for him. I wanted so much to tell him my feelings, but all I could utter was a soft, "Charlie." My grasp of the English language was still too inadequate to properly express my heartfelt sorrow at what he went through in the POW camps still going through his mind. All I wanted was to take Charlie in my arms and comfort him, to erase all the pain from his memory, and to let him know that I truly cared for him. I realized that my tears were streaming down my face and falling in small puddles on my plate. Somehow we managed to get up from the table and walk out of the restaurant. All the way back to Bien Hoa, however, neither of us muttered a sound, each engrossed in our own thought.

Chapter 6

A Dream Comes True

On August 18, 1969, the biggest day of my life had finally arrived. My faith took wing and soared all the way to heaven. God was fulfilling my most cherished dream—the dream of a métisse from Indochina to meet her father in a faraway place and to feel his love.

Charlie picked me up at my house. At the door, he found me in the midst of my tearful family, wishing me a bon voyage and giving me last-minute advice. "If you get lost or cannot find your father, go to the closest *gendarme* (French policeman) for help." Our maid was also worried. She gave me a big hug and made me promise not to get lost.

Naturally, I was excited and a bit afraid at first, but my faith in God and my joy of finding my father soon overcame my fear. We arrived at Tan Son Nhut Airport at 5:00 p.m., and my plane was scheduled to leave at 6:00. Charlie and I had only a few minutes together, which we spent in each other's arms.

After a long kiss Charlie sent me on my way with, "Have a safe trip, sweetie. I love you."

"Thank you for everything, Charlie. I shall return soon."

During the long flight, our plane made stops in Bangkok, Bombay, Calcutta, and Athens. After twenty-two long hours we finally touched down at Orly Airport in Paris at 7:30 a.m. A bad case of nervousness suddenly appeared as the plane came to a complete stop. Was this a beginning or an end? In just moments I would be meeting the man I had always dreamed of meeting someday. Should I call him "Papa" just as any child would? Or should I be more formal and call him...what? My mind was in a frenzy of questions.

I walked from the plane to the terminal building. Immediately, the public announcement system called "Mademoiselle Yvonne Roullain, please report to the information desk." I came face-to-face with a tall, distinguished-looking man, impeccably dressed in a black suit, who was staring directly at me. I wanted to walk faster, but my feet felt as though they were bound by leg irons around my ankles.

"Papa! Je suis très contente de vous voir!" (Father, I am very happy to see you!) I exclaimed joyously.

I turned toward the attractive lady standing next to him, who I knew to be my stepmother Paulette, and gave her a big hug also. "Je vous remercie pour m'accepter" (Thank you both for accepting me).

As we walked toward their car, Papa asked about my grandfather and the rest of the family in Vietnam. At a nice sidewalk café in Paris we ate a delicious breakfast of croissants and coffee.

"Yvonne," Papa said, "you will need to rest for the trip back to our home at Saint Genis Pouilly, because we will not arrive there until around eight o'clock tonight. Our home is close to the Swiss border, so the ride will be somewhat of an ordeal after your long flight. There will be a special treat for you when we get there, though, for your sister Monique will have a welcome-home dinner ready for us." Then, as an afterthought, he continued, "The next time you come, your flight should be routed to Geneva, Switzerland, since it is much closer." With only a couple of stops for lunch and a brief rest, we made the trip from Paris to Saint Genis. All the way I enjoyed the lovely, breathtaking scenery. Papa's home was an elegant, two-story house sturdily-built of brick to withstand several generations of Bouttoirs. Downstairs was a comfortable, sunken living room with a large fireplace, a formal-yet-inviting dining room, a cozy eat-in kitchen, and a small bathroom. Three spacious bedrooms with vaulted ceilings and a bathroom completed the upstairs.

Upon our arrival, my sister Monique greeted us, along with her husband and close family friends. Since this was a special occasion, Paulette's mother, Grandma, also joined us. My brother Paul could not be there since he was in the French military.

Our dinner that evening reminded me of the ones we had in the French compound when I was four years old. An apéritif (before dinner drink) and wine from Papa's wine cave were served to celebrate our reunion. The meal consisted of soup, hor d'oeuvres, lamb, potato casserole, spinach soufflé, sautéed carrots, a salad, cheese, and rum cake for dessert. The appropriate liqueur followed. I felt very special because Monique prepared such an elaborate meal for my homecoming.

A very elegant room awaited me upstairs. Even though it was late, I stayed up to write letters to my mother and Charlie. The next morning I enjoyed the view of the Swiss Alps from my bedroom window. I was so thankful to be here and so excited. Although it was very early, I tiptoed down the stairs to find Papa already up and making coffee.

"Bonjour, Papa," I greeted him. This was the first time I ever got the chance to tell my father "good morning."

"Bonjour, Yvonne. Did you sleep well?"

"I didn't sleep much because I felt so good all over," I admitted. He smiled. We sat down together and drank coffee and talked for a while. I asked his permission to send a telegram to Charlie to let him know that I arrived safely and found my papa.

"Of course." He looked very happy. "We've planned a trip for next week. First we shall visit with your brother Paul and then go on to Italy."

When I met Paul, I found him to be as warm and loving as Monique. He, too, hugged me, making me feel very special and close to him.

During my stay at Papa's home, Monique took me to Geneva several times to go shopping. Before we left for Italy Grandma gave me some money for shopping. What a thoughtful, sweet woman!

The time came to go to Italy. Papa, Paulette, and another couple and their two daughters and I left Saint Genis Pouilly in the afternoon and drove to Switzerland. There we spent the night in a beautiful hotel. The two girls and I shared a room. The snow-covered Swiss countryside and the majestic Alps were beautiful. It was the first time I had ever seen snow, and I delightfully enjoyed playing in it.

Late in the afternoon of the second day of our trip, we checked into the Hannover Hotel in Jesolo Lido, Italy. Again, the girls and I shared a room. During the day we went to the beach. At night we visited the sidewalk cafés and ice cream shops in downtown Jesolo Lido. All along the streets we noticed pretty Italian girls singing to the music playing inside the various sidewalk shops.

During our stay I bought gifts for my family, as well as for Charlie. Papa and my stepmother surprised me with a big, beautiful doll to remember our time together in Italy.

Two days later we traveled to Venezia (Venice) by boat, where we visited St. Marcus Basilica, Ducal Palace, St. Georgia Island, Nocturn, and a number of other interesting sights, with thousands of pigeons serving as our unofficial tour guides. In one palace we saw Roman clothes, suits of armor, and many paintings. Our tour guides, who were all multi-lingual, explained the meaning of each relic as well as its historical significance. The history really impressed me. Since I love to read and write, I found all this information fascinating.

Along the sidewalks of Venezia, I noticed many old women crocheting sweaters and other items of clothing that they apparently sold to shops, who in turn sold them to the tourists. As a result, sweaters and clothes were very reasonably priced. However, I bought Charlie a beautiful set of glasses. Before we left Venezia and returned to Jesolo Lido, we ate a seafood dinner on the water. They served the fish whole without filleting them. Just the way I liked my seafood.

Everyone was exhausted when we got back to the Hannover Hotel. I took a shower then spent the rest of the evening writing to Mother and Charlie. I told Charlie that the waitresses always served us a plate of spaghetti with each order whether we wanted it or not.

With all the excitement, however, the most enjoyable moments of my trip had been the time I spent with my father.

"How is you mother?" he asked.

"She has a little problem with her health," I replied.

"What kind of health problem?"

"She has chronic asthma."

"Does she take any medication for it?"

"Yes, but it doesn't seem to help much."

All too soon our two-week vacation in Italy was over. When we got back to Saint Genis Pouilly, Papa and I recounted each day and each moment we spent together. He said that one month was not enough. He was certainly right. How could we catch up with our lives and all the things we had missed for twenty-one years in just one month?

Papa took Monique and me to Geneva to shop for the last time before I had to return to Vietnam. Monique bought a cuckoo clock for me as a souvenir.

Then it was bon voyage time again. I hoped fervently that it was not adieu. Papa gave me the money for the airfare back to Vietnam as he had promised. As he helped me pack my suitcase, neither of us could conceal our emotions. We could not help the way we felt. We were both so very thankful for this long-awaited reunion. Through our faith we had found one another.

Papa, Paulette, and Grandma took me to Paris the day before my scheduled departure. Papa wanted to show me around Paris, especially the Eiffel Tower, Notre Dame, and the Champ de Elysees. Paris is a romantic place. That night Grandma and I shared a hotel room. She was so sweet, and I really liked her.

When we arrived at the airport the next morning, I started crying. " Dear God," I prayed, "why do I always have to say goodbye to the ones I love?" Then Papa began to cry too. He kept repeating to me, "*À bientôt, à bientôt*, Yvonne" (See you soon, Yvonne).

They stayed with me as long as they could. When we finally had to part I gave Papa one more big hug, holding him tight for a long time. I did not want to let him go for fear of losing him. Again I was reminded of when the French were in Vietnam fifteen years earlier, when I had to bid Captain Pouley adieu.

As soon as I entered the airplane, I became violently ill and made several trips to the bathroom to vomit. During the next twenty-two hours of flying, I could not eat. The only thing that stayed in my stomach was Seven Up. Apparently the emotional strain was too much for me.

Charlie was at the airport to greet me with a broad smile. "Did you have a good trip, sweetheart? I really missed you. I thought you would never come back."

"I am here," I replied, "and I missed you too." I was so happy to see Charlie, and in just one more hour I would see Mother. I had missed her terribly. Charlie drove me home and left immediately. I thanked him and told him that I would see him at the office in the morning.

My family greeted me at the door, excited at my homecoming. They wanted to know everything about my father and the trip. We stayed up until 2:00 a.m. that night, talking about my trip and catching up on the news. I gave everyone their gifts, including our maid. I handed Mother whatever money I had not spent on my trip, along with the Chanel Number Five perfume, and promised her that I would love her and take care of her.

The next morning I returned to work. Charlie and I had breakfast together. Our relationship was growing stronger every day. My family now permitted me to spend Sundays from 10:00 a.m. until 5:00 p.m. with Charlie, which never seemed like enough time to us. Every Sunday morning Charlie would teach me how to drive. Then we would return to my house, and I would prepare lunch for us. We did not go out because I was afraid the neighbors would get the wrong idea about a Vietnamese girl dating an American.

There were a few young Vietnamese women who worked in our office. From time to time, they would tell Charlie, "Yvonne doesn't love you, or she would spend a night with you." At first Charlie believed them, but he eventually realized that I had been raised differently than they. Those young women were free to do whatever they wished.

I often thought of Ben, but I also realized that my feelings had increased for Charlie. I knew that it was not good to love both men, therefore, I decided to stop writing to Ben.

Chapter 7

A Promise

On Thanksgiving Day 1969, Charlie and I had to work. We traveled to Phouc Long Province for an emergency meeting. Unfortunately we had our Thanksgiving dinner with the advisors of the province. In the middle of our meal we received an urgent radio call from the pilot of the plane that was scheduled to pick us up that we must leave immediately.

As soon as we boarded the plane, the pilot explained that the Viet Cong were attacking all around the area. "Say a prayer. We might not make it," he said. The take-off was frightening. We could not go all the way to the end of the runway else we might have gotten hit from enemy fire. Since Phouc Long's airport was noted for its especially short landing strip anyway, the ordeal was even scarier. As the plane began its fast take-off, Charlie turned around in his seat and looked me straight in the eyes and reached for my left hand. "Will you marry me if we get back safely?"

"Yes," I quickly replied. "And I will always love you and take care of you." This moment meant a lot to both of us, especially in such time of danger.

After our narrow escape and return to the relative safety of the office, Charlie filled out an application to the State Department in Washington for permission for us to get married. The approval took several months, causing my family and us unimaginable frustration. My family withheld its permission for me to marry Charlie, not because he was an American, but because of our age difference. He was twenty-seven years older than I. Besides, a friend had introduced me to a Vietnamese lawyer of whom the family approved and expected me to marry after I finished college. Frequently my family commented, "We have two teachers, a nurse, two restaurant owners, some high-ranking military officers, and we would like to have a lawyer." It was a difficult time for me. "I love Charlie," was the only reply I would give them. Many times I asked myself, "Why do I love Charlie? Is it because I miss my father's love?"

At last my family gave their approval for our marriage. Charlie finally received a telegram from Washington signed by Secretary of State Rogers approving the union. It was the ambassador's understanding that the future Mrs. Combs would not reside in Vietnam. This was good and bad news. First, I would have to resign from my job. Second, after we were married I would have to leave Vietnam for safe-haven housing.

On March 1, 1970, we left Saigon for the United States, to be married in Missouri. That night we stopped over in Hong Kong. After checking into our room at the President Hotel, Charlie showered and dressed for dinner while I rested in a comfortable easy chair. When it was my turn to use the bathroom, Charlie quietly excused himself and went down to the dining room to reserve us a table for dinner. While waiting for me to join him, he ordered himself a scotch and water, which he sipped slowly as he glanced intermittently toward the staircase. He did not want to drink too much for fear he would ruin the pleasant evening he had planned for the two of us.

About thirty minutes later, Charlie spied me standing at the top of the stairs. His eye never left mine as I slowly descended down the long, winding stairs. I had changed into a long, simple black gown that revealed every twist and turn of my slim body. I could tell by the gleam in Charlie's eyes that my entrance had a stunning effect on him. As I reached the table Charlie stood up and walked over to my side, pulling out the chair for me. Seating himself once more, he signaled the waiter and ordered me a glass of orange juice.

We didn't say much for the next few minutes. We just looked into each other's eyes and held hands. Then Charlie reached into the pocket of his gray pinstripe suit and pulled out a small black velvet box. When he opened it up I gasped at an exquisite two-and-one-half carat diamond ring. He placed the ring on my finger and said, "I love you, Yvonne."

The song "In the Still of the Night" was playing, and Charlie asked me to dance. As my eyes rested for a brief moment on his, I could see in his eyes that he wanted to hold me close to his heart and whisper to me the strange secrets of its passionate history. All thoughts and all passion soon merged into that one, all-consuming desire I could see from the depths of the most passionate of hearts. I felt like a flower that had sprung up in the desert and shed its fragrance over my life, made its ways attractive with its beauty, and turned its weariness to contentment with its sweet spirit.

I felt our lips moving closer and closer together while the song "In the Still of the Night" played once again. After the dance we returned to our table and ordered a light supper of fish and vegetables. We finished our dinner and the next morning boarded a flight to Hawaii before continuing on to the United States.

When we arrived at the airport in Kansas City, Missouri, Charlie's mother Maude and his brother Shorty met us at the arrival gate. After Charlie exchanged a big hug with his family he introduced me to his mother. "Mom, this is Yvonne."I bowed to show respect, while she reached out to pull me to her for a hug. "I'm glad to meet you, Yvonne."

Maude looked much younger than her age and appeared quite healthy for a seventy-two-year-old woman. Shorty, who was seven years older than Charlie, had been in the carnival business most of his life. Although his work was difficult and he had led a rough life, Shorty had a wonderful sense of humor. From the time we got into the car until we reached Maude's house, Shorty entertained us with all sorts of jokes. The long drive from Kansas City to Blairstown took us three hours because of the snow and ice that covered much of the roads, but Shorty seemed not notice the hazardous conditions. He was too busy talking and joking.

One of his favorite jokes was: "A dignified, well-respected old gentleman died and went to heaven. St. Peter met him at the pearly gates and after a cursory review of his splendid record, informed the old man that he was to be awarded a chauffeur-driven limousine twenty-four hours a day, indefinitely, to go anywhere he so desired. The man thanked St. Peter and departed. A few days later, St. Peter was making his rounds when he discovered the limousine parked at the side of the road with the old man leaning over the hood, crying like a baby. St. Peter rushed over and inquired as to what could cause such grief. The man replied in sobs that he just saw his wife going down the road on a bicycle." We really enjoyed his jokes.

We arrived at Maude's farm late in the afternoon. By then Charlie and I were certainly feeling the jet lag. Maude immediately began preparing the evening meal and, even though I was exhausted, I offered to help her. Where I come from, we had to prepare the meal and make the tea for the mother-in-law. When supper was ready, Maude kept telling me, "Sit down."

I was very uncomfortable. I waited for her to sit down at the table first. This was the way we were taught to respect the mother-in-law. After dinner, I cleaned up the table and volunteered to wash the dishes. Charlie and I then went out in the backyard to see the camper in which we would be spending the night. It was very small, but very cozy and private. We returned to the house and looked at the family picture albums until Maude served us fresh, steaming cups of coffee and deliciously rich chocolate cream pie. I paid very close attention while she prepared the pie, asking all sorts of question about the recipe so that I could make pie for my husband after we were married. I knew Charlie liked chocolate pie.

We had a good night's rest, and it was my first night on a farm in America. After a hearty breakfast the next morning, we began to make plans for our wedding. The local preacher we contacted to perform the wedding was reluctant, because we were not members of his flock or of his denomination. Although we were disappointed, we continued to search.

A few days later a local Baptist minister from a neighboring city agreed to perform the ceremony. Maude insisted that the wedding be held in her house, so preparations began.

The major problem, however, was Maude's pet myna bird, Elmer, talked all the time and cursed like a drunken sailor. Maude decided that she would move Elmer from the kitchen into the back room and cover his cage with a sheet during the ceremony. The preacher arrived about 6:00 p.m. and the ceremony started one hour later. The preacher, who was hard of hearing, could not remember my maiden name.

"What did you say your name was?" he asked in the middle of the ceremony. After repeating my name over and over again, it became comical. Everyone there started to snicker. Elmer started screeching in his cage and cursing in a low voice, which stopped the proceedings. The minister stopped and looked around the room to see why everyone was giggling. Maude had mistakenly thought that Elmer would fall asleep once his cage was covered, but that did not happen. Fortunately the clergyman never heard him or discovered why we were giggling. After he left we all had a good laugh over the whole matter.

On March 16 we exchanged vows in front of God: "For better, for worse, for richer, for poorer, in sickness and in health, to love and to cherish, till death do us part." This vow was important to me, and I promised myself I would obey God's law.

After the ceremony we had ice cream and cake. Charlie and his family exchanged a few jokes, and then we excused ourselves to go to the camper where we would spend our honeymoon.

When we got into the camper, Charlie fell asleep after a brief conversation with me. I lay there on the bed next to him waiting for him to do something, but nothing happened. We did not make love on our first wedding night. Even though Charlie was my husband now, I was still very shy. I did not try to wake him up or complain. I just lay there very still, concerned that maybe this was a sign of bad luck coming our way for our marriage and we might have to sleep in separate bedrooms for the rest of our married life.

I remembered when I was twelve years old and I witnessed my aunt's wedding. It was very interesting. The Vietnamese wedding, which is usually fixed by reference to the horoscope and usually falls a couple of months after the betrothal, is a simple ritual amounting to little more than a presentation of the groom and the bride to the ancestors. An intermediary informs the ancestors of the marriage, and the bride and groom kneel before the ancestral altar. Then, in order of precedence beginning with the groom's elder male kin, the couple kneels before their assembled relatives. The bride's parents, however, are absent, for their presence at the ceremony is considered to be unlucky. Gift giving and feasting by the guests follow the ritual. After all the guest have departed, the newly-joined pair pass to the bridal chamber which, by tradition, the bride must enter first, lest she step on her husband's shadow and cause him to come under her domination throughout their married life.

The next morning we woke up in each other's arms. Charlie gave me a kiss.

"Mrs. Combs, you don't have to make coffee this morning."

"Neither do you, Mr. Combs."

Even though it was our honeymoon, I tried to help Maude with everything I could lay my hands on. Not only was she my mother-in-law but she was also seventy-two years old. I could not just sit there and let the old folks do all the work.

The snow was still deep and the temperature frigid in Blairstown, Missouri, in the middle of March. The small community had a population of about 175 people, mostly elderly farmers who retired early each night after their favorite television program, *Hee Haw*. Charlie and I were just like two little birds trying to find a warm nest on our honeymoon, which we spent in the camper parked in my new mother-in-law's backyard on the farm she owned.

Every day I went fishing or rabbit hunting with Charlie. He taught me how to shoot. I even tried milking a cow. Charlie made it look so easy, but even with both hands I was not very successful.

Chapter 8

Return to the Motherland

Our honeymoon was over when our thirty-day leave ended. Charlie and I had to return to Vietnam, where I found my mother ill, so we sent a letter to USAID to request an extended leave for me. It was approved. Before we were married I explained to Charlie that I had promised my mother and myself that I would care for her the rest of her life, and she would be with me wherever I might go.

As Charlie's wife I was now able to move into State Department housing. I told Charlie I would like to have children, but was disappointed month after month. My cousin, a nurse, suggested that I should not think about it and then it would happen.

On July 19 I returned from the doctor's office ecstatic. I had finally conceived. Throughout the pregnancy I touched my stomach and talked to my baby. From the very start I felt close to my unborn child and loved it deeply. I began reading baby books to learn how to be a good mother. I continued to cook all of Charlie's favorite exotic dishes for him until my fourth month. Just the smell of spicy foods made me sick, so I had to train the maid to cook. Mother also helped a lot since she was now living with us. Following the Vietnamese customs, I did not wear high heels, walk fast, or lift anything during my pregnancy, nor did I smoke or drink. Every day I read books, listened to soft music, and treated my husband with a pleasant face and kissed him at the door when he came home from work.

One evening Charlie brought home a memorandum from the personnel office informing us that I had to leave Vietnam. Prior to my marriage to Charlie, I was a native of Vietnam. When we got married, my status changed to a dependent of a U.S. citizen who was working in a combat zone. At my request, Charlie wrote a letter to them requesting an extension of leave, because I was expecting a child. Fortunately, our request was approved.

As time went by I got the feeling that I would have a boy. The Vietnamese can usually tell what the sex of the baby will be by looking at the shape of the mother's stomach and what the woman likes to eat during her pregnancy. I started to crochet sweaters and hats in blue. I never stopped talking to my son and telling him how much I loved him, just like my mother loved me. Mother told me that when Papa came home from work each evening he would kiss her stomach where she carried me. I thanked my mother for breast-feeding me for my first thirteen months of life.

On March 26, 1971, I brought into this world a beautiful baby boy, who we named Christopher. There was no greater joy in my life. I held my child in my arms, loved him, and vowed to protect him from all the tragedies in life. My mother remained at the hospital with me for two weeks, taking care of Chris for me. I rested and followed all the Vietnamese customs I was supposed to follow—taking long, relaxing baths with herbs; lying down on the bed while the maid washed my hair; placing the heating pad on my stomach; and sitting over a little charcoal stove of roasting whole peppers for healing. I did not eat anything sour for six months because the Vietnamese believe that sour food will make a woman's menstrual flow much heavier. High-heeled shoes were still a no-no, because they were bad for the veins, and intercourse should not take place for three months. I followed all those rules diligently.

Our family happiness lasted until we received another memorandum from the American Embassy demanding that Chris and I leave Vietnam for safe haven in Bangkok, Thailand. Now, when I really needed my family, I had to leave my husband, my mother, and the rest of my family behind in Vietnam while my infant and I relocated to a new, strange country. So much for the United States Department of State rule that allows no dependents in a combat zone, regardless of the fact that they are natives.

Charlie accompanied Chris and me to Bangkok on November 1. The State Department housing there was very nice. Our apartment even had living quarters for a maid. The food and climate were very much like Vietnam's. Charlie stayed with us five days and then returned to Vietnam. Each month the U.S. government allowed Charlie five days of leave from Vietnam to spend with us in Bangkok.

Before I left Vietnam for Thailand Charlie gave me two thousand dollars, which he had converted to local currency, totaling almost one million piasters. I gave that money to my mother to purchase a nice home or to live on for a long time. I was so thankful for Charlie's generosity.

Every morning I would put Chris in his stroller and wheel him down the streets of Bangkok to the morning market on Sukumvit Road, where I would buy fresh fruit and vegetables. I used my money wisely. Charlie gave me two hundred dollars a month. I saved one hundred dollars to send to my mother. Every day I wrote to both my mother and Charlie.

Although I missed them terribly, I had to control my emotions and not let them know just how much I hated being there without them. I even wrote to Ben once to let him know that I had married and was now living in Bangkok. Since I was now married and intended to remain loyal to my husband, I decided to burn all Ben's letters and pictures, except the one I had kept in my *English for Today* book. I had to close that chapter in my life.

The first month dragged by slowly until the day I went to the airport to pick up Charlie. It felt like six months instead of just one. When he got off the plane I ran to greet him, so happy that we were together again. We returned to our apartment and I prepared lunch for us. That night we checked into the Dusi-Tani Hotel, where we watched the Miss Universe Pageant that was being held there.

Each evening we attended a different, exciting place, such as Chao Pyah; Choc Chai's Steak House. During the day the two of us took Chris to either the morning market on Sukumvit Road or the floating market. With Charlie, life in Bangkok was very exciting. But all too soon, the five days of leave were gone, and Charlie had to return to Vietnam. Before he left, Charlie told me that he had requested a transfer to Laos so Chris and I could be with him.

On December 5 he called to tell me that he had an interview in Vientiane, Laos, two days later. I prayed that his transfer would go through. Thank God, He answered my prayers. Now the three of us would be together again. We arrived in Vientiane on February 3, 1972, and stayed in the city for two weeks, waiting for all the paperwork to be completed for Charlie's new assignment at Luang Prabang—the Kingdom of Laos.

Fortunately, all the USAID/RO people in Vientiane were exceptionally nice, just like one big, happy family. They welcomed us as if we were another addition to their already large clan, especially Mr. and Mrs. John Hogg, Charlie's new boss and his wife. They were a wonderful couple.

Mr. and Mrs. Hogg picked us up at the airport in Vientiane

and gave us a royal welcome. They took us to their home, prepared a delicious meal, and furnished us a room to spend the night. The following morning we were fed a hearty breakfast and Mr. Hogg made arrangements for our housing. I will always remember their kindness and generosity.

After we settled down in our new home and Charlie settled into his new position, we set out to get to know this country and its people. For our first adventure, Charlie, Chris, and I visited the wats (temples) of Vientiane. What an interesting and enlightening experience. It enabled us to understand and appreciate the importance of Buddhism to the Laotian people. The wats were open every weekend and during Buddhist holidays. Courtesy required that visitors remove their shoes before entering these national shrines.

"According to the booklets we received, there are three most interesting wats in Vientiane. Wat Phra Keo, Wat Sisaket, and Wat Luang. Which one do you want to go see?" Charlie asked.

"We don't know our way around. We will go see which one we can find. Did it say where they are located in the book?" I asked.

"According to this, Wat Phra Keo is in the palace grounds opposite the Mahosot Hospital. We know where the hospital is."

Wat Phra Keo was originally built in 1565 by King Setthathirath. In 1936 the government restored the temple and made it a national museum. The Era Wan, the God Indra's three headed elephant, was carved above the main doors. Phra Keo, or Green God, refers to the Emerald Buddha, which is now in the Wat Phra Keo in Bangkok. The museum contains Buddha images of many different historical periods.

Buddhas can be found in many different poses—standing, walking, sitting, or reclining. The seated Buddha with his right arm pointed earthward represents the powerful deity who overcomes evil. Interior murals depict scenes from the life of Buddha as well as elephants. Elephants are greatly revered in this country. In fact, their national flag has three elephants on it.

In addition to visiting the wats and other landmarks during our two-week stay in Vientiane, Charlie and I also discovered several delicious French cuisines, particularly escargot, which was out of this world!

On February 20 we arrived at Luang Prabang, Charlie's new assignment. Luang Prabang, located about 160 kilometers north of Vientiane, is the royal capital of Laos. Bob Reynold, who Charlie would be working with, picked us up at the airport. "I'm Bob. Welcome to Luang Prabang."

"I'm glad to meet you, Bob. This is my wife, Yvonne."

"It's nice to meet you, Yvonne." We shook hands.

"How is everything here, Bob?" Charlie asked.

"It has been quiet so far, but we keep our eyes on it. I would like to take you and Yvonne for a quick tour before we go to your house."

"We would appreciate that," Charlie said.

Bob explained to us as he drove along. "This is the morning market where you can buy fresh vegetables, fruit, and meat, though I don't advise you to buy the meat from the market. Once a month we have our own pilot fly us in the C47 airplane to NKB (a military base) in Thailand for the commissary and the PX."

"It's good to know," Charlie said.

"In this street in front of these stores is where they have their evening market. They usually sell sweets such as coconut custard, coconut sticky rice, and coconut bananas. They put coconut in most of their food."

"Is that right?" Charlie said.

"Yes. You and Yvonne ought to try some of it sometime. It tastes pretty good."

Bob pointed his finger as he turned. "This is King Savant Vatthana's Palace." Charlie and I looked in the direction Bob's finger pointed. We both stared in amazement.

"Looks like the gardener is busy with the queen's flower garden," I said. The flower garden really impressed me. I had enjoyed flowers and exotic plants of all species since I was six years old. I couldn't imagine anything more beautiful than a well-maintained flower garden.

"You and Yvonne probably already know that their flag has three elephants on it," Bob commented.

"Yes, we noticed when we were in Vientiane. There must be a history behind the elephants," Charlie said.

Bob said, "One of the stories I was told is that for most Laotians, merely being there evokes a sense of awe. Not only is it the residence of their sovereign but also the historical center of Laos, known as Lane Xang.

"Buddhism, the state religion, had its beginnings in this city, which is named for the Prabang, a sacred Buddha image that, according to legend, had been cast by the pious fold of Ceylon from gold bracelets, diamond rings, silver, copper, iron objects, precious stones, and pewter. Centuries earlier as the Buddhist doctrine spread eastward from Ceylon, this statue was brought to Ankor in Cambodia.

"At the same time, Fa Ngum, the young son of a Laos Chieftan, lived as an exile in Ankor under the care and tutelage of a scholarly monk. When the prince turned sixteen the king of the Khmera gave Fa Ngum his daughter's hand in marriage and provided him with a large army, in order that the prince might regain his position in the Laos state. Fa Ngum succeeded in reconquering his father's former territories, and in 1353 he set himself upon the throne, which he called Lane Xang, or 'Lord of the million elephants,' in what is present-day Luang Prabang."

"This is very interesting. History always fascinates me," I said.

"We're going to turn left here. I want to show you where the prince lives."

"He doesn't live in the king's palace?" Charlie asked.

"No. In fact, I've seen him once in a while in his black Mercedes," Bob said.

We drove about ten minutes; then Bob stopped and said, "We cannot go beyond this point—not only for us Americans, but also for the Laotians."

"I see the big red flag," Charlie said.

"The Laotians know it is a restricted area, but a few of them still risk their lives to find the elephant tusks. They have been killed by the Khmer Rouge."

When I heard Bob say, "Khmer Rouge," I thought about when I was in Vietnam and lived under the conditions of war. I never knew when I might get killed by the Viet Cong, but I did not fear death. Death is not to be feared, but used as a reminder of the real meaning of life. Therefore we should live each day to the full as if there will be no tomorrow. The test is not how long one has lived, but how *much* one has lived. I have lived more than most could even partially attain, and it is simply because I believe it is worth it. One day will come when that will not be so, but I do not fear it.

There are always a few good memories from each and every day if we only look. Beauty is where one finds it.

Then Bob took us to our place. The United States government provided us with a three-bedroom house, plus living quarters for the maid. Most importantly, however, they provided us with a constant guard, which made me feel much safer.

The next day Bob introduced the maids to us. They bowed and said, "Mister; Madame." I hired both of them—one for housekeeping and the other for babysitting.

We also employed a male cook who had worked for the French for many years and came highly recommended.

It took us a few weeks to get everything organized. We were still waiting for our household effects to arrive from Bangkok.

On April 8 Charlie brought home an invitation that was written in French from the king and queen of the royal palace.

"I read the card, but I didn't understand what it says. Did you notice the top of the card?" Charlie asked.

"No," I replied.

"Hold up the card. You'll see the three elephant heads."

"Yes, I see them."

On April 15 Charlie and I, along with other members of the State Department, attended the New Year (Pi Mai) celebration at the king's palace. Pi Mai, which commemorates the ending of the old year and the beginning of the new, takes place in April every year.

We arrived at the king's palace at 7:40 p.m. and proceeded immediately to pay our respects to the king and queen. Several pretty Laotian girls accompanied the royal couple, carrying large silver urns filled with flowers. As the royal entourage made its way through the multitude of guests, the people sprinkled them with perfumed water.

The traditional dance was performed. Two dancers wearing strawlike coats and gay, red lacquer masks that gave them the appearance of gods represented the first Lao male and female. After the dance ended they bowed to their king and offered him the best wishes of all the Laos—present, past, and future.

In the middle of the room stood a long table loaded with all kinds of exotic foods, both Laotian and French gourmet. Soft, beautiful music played while attractive women dressed in luxurious, flowing gowns waltzed with their handsome escorts, adding even more festivity to the atmosphere of the palace. Charlie and I had our first waltz in the king's palace.

Directly behind the palace toward a ten thousand-foot mountain was a line of more than one thousand Lao school children. Each carried a flaming torch as they slowly wound their way down the mountain trail to depict the dance of the dragon.

The next day we also had the great honor of attending a special ceremony at Prince Heritien Vong Savong Palace. For someone who had read many books about such grandeur and splendor and could only hope to dream about it, I was part of it all. It was an experience I would remember and cherish for the rest of my life.

Charlie and I enjoyed our stay in Luang Prabang. Most of all, we enjoyed just being together with Chris.

Charlie bought me a cute little white Fiat sports car, which I used to travel to the market every morning for fresh fruits and vegetables. The Laotian people were very polite and respectful, although very few of the maids spoke English. I had to learn enough of their language to communicate effectively with the servants as well as with the vendors at the market. I had great compassion for the servants and often gave them American food, extra pay, or fabric for them to make their clothes. They took very good care of me. Our maid would massage my back with fragrant oil each afternoon and give me a manicure and pedicure once a week.

Even though we lived well, I missed my mother dreadfully and constantly worried about her safety.

I told Chris sometimes when I was playing with him, "Grandma misses us so much, and we miss Grandma, too."

When I could stand being away from her no longer, I said to Charlie, "I would like to take Chris with me to visit my mother for one month if that is all right with you."

"It's all right, but we have to attend the U.S. ambassador and his wife's party on May 8."

"Where is the invitation card?"

"It's on the table. Didn't you read it?"

I walked over to the table to get the card and read it. "We have to go to Vientiane for this one," I remarked.

"That will give you a chance to eat some more of that good escargot."

"Sounds good!" I exclaimed. "We have to bring the maid to watch Chris."

"Certainly, and I have to call Vientiane to arrange a guest house for us."

Charlie and I traveled to Vientiane to attend the ambassador and his wife's party on May 8. I told Charlie that I was impressed with the charm and beauty of the ambassador's wife.

"She is probably from Greece. Did you see the white cat she has?" Charlie inquired.

"Yes, I did. It is a beautiful cat, probably expensive too."

The party was a gala affair, an experience I would remember forever.

One week later Chris and I left for Vietnam. Charlie arranged for his pilot to take the two of us from Luang Prabang to Vientiane. That part of the trip was extremely frightening—flying in a small, twin-engine plane across rugged mountains with the possibility of going down in such inhospitable terrain. Fortunately my love for Mother overcame my fear. I just held my son close to me and thought of the happy moment when we would be reunited with her. From Vientiane to Saigon we flew on Royal Air Laos. My heart was trembling when the plane finally came to a complete stop at Tan Son Nhut Airport.

"Yvonne!" my mother called as I was checking through customs. I looked up and saw several members of my family anxiously waiting. I waved to Mother, Uncle, Aunt, and cousins. Although it had been only a few months since we had not seen each other, it felt more like several years. My family was delighted with Chris. He was so cute. Since my uncle was a commander in the Vietnamese navy, he took us all through the gate at Tan Son Nhut without any problems. After exchanging hugs and kisses we all went to the floating restaurant at Bach Dang Bay for dinner. We spent the night at Uncle's house. The next morning he took us on to Bien Hoa.

When we arrived home, Aunt Maria was sitting in the divan by the door. I ran and gave her a big hug.

"I am so happy to see you. I thought of you often," I said.

"We all missed you too. I know it must have been difficult for you, because you worried about your mother."

"Yes, I worried and missed her a lot. I'm going to try to bring her with me to Laos."

I was so happy to see my Aunt Maria once again. Everyone in our family respected and loved her, because she was truly a great person in our eyes. All her life she had taken care of her family—first her parents, followed by her sisters, and then her nieces. She admired me, too, because of my love and devotion to my mother. For my homecoming, Aunt prepared all my favorite foods—catfish cooked with pineapple, white bamboo shoots, watercress cooked with pork brain soup, fried bullhead (another type of catfish) cooked very crispy, bouillabaisse, and broiled stuffed shrimp on sugar cane.

The following day I started visiting my other relatives. At the market several friends were happy to see me, as I had been gone for several months. Everyone knew my family and me. All my ancestors had been born and raised in Bien Hoa. They were even buried there.

Two days later I went to Saigon to apply for an exit visa so mother could accompany Chris and me to Laos. Someone at the Ministry of the Interior informed me that no one was allowed to travel at that time except American dependents. I was disappointed, but I had always believed in myself. Now I just had to find a way. It came to me. Money. That was the key.

I returned to Luang Prabang after promising Mother that I would come back and get her out of Vietnam. When I got back Charlie told me he had been transferred to Savannakhet, so we had to move again. The U.S. government moved us with a C-130 cargo plane in one load—all our personal effects, my car, Charlie's truck, the maid, the dog, and us. Savannakhet lies two hundred fifty kilometers south of Vientiane on the Mekong River. It was the second largest city in Laos with a population of almost thirty-six thousand.

I liked our new surroundings better than Luang Prabang. Once again the government had provided us with a beautiful home and excellent maid's quarters.

We had been in Savannakhet only a few days when we attended the area coordinator's party at his home, followed the next day by a party at the home of a Lao colonel. At least twice a week Charlie and I attended parties or private dinners. Both the Americans and the Laotians treated us wonderfully. We became like family. Everyone was far from home, and we tried to make the best of it in this foreign country. Danger remained ever present, because we never knew when we might be killed by the Khmer Rouge.

The area that we were in was known as the Iron Triangle. Laos, Vietnam, and Cambodia were all joined a short distance away. The Ho Chi Minh Trail also crossed at this triangle of three countries.

After a few months in Savannakhet Chris and I returned

to Vietnam. This time we took Royal Air Laos directly from Savannakhet to Saigon. Mother was surprised that I had come back so soon. I explained that the reason for my quick return was to take her back to Laos with me.

"It is impossible now, my daughter," she said.

"Mother," I replied, " all my life I have believed in myself and that I would make it. Please have faith in me."

I sold my diamond bracelet and my big engagement ring that Charlie bought for me in Hong Kong so I could get enough money to bribe an exit visa for my mother. Although I had previously written several letters to the Vietnamese Ministry about this matter, they never replied.

One afternoon when I was feeding Chris, I heard a man's voice asking, "Is Minh home?" Turning towards him, I said, "Hello. No, I am sorry, but he is not home." After a few minutes of conversation, he informed me that he worked for General Hiep in Saigon.

"Can the general arrange an exit visa for my mother?" I asked.

"The general only has to make a phone call," he replied.

"How much?"

"One hundred thousand piasters."

"OK. You talk to him and get back with me." I looked at him in earnest.

Cousin Minh arrived home and noticed my guest. "Hi, Brother Vinh. Maybe you can help Yvonne with her mother's exit visa."

"We have already discussed it," I told Minh, who explained to me that General Hiep was a husband to one of our distant cousins. Her father was my grand aunt's nephew. "Really?" The thought crossed my mind that sometimes having a relative in a position of power is a mixed blessing. It could be good or bad, depending upon the attitude and thinking of those in power.

Three days later Vinh came back to Bien Hoa for the money. I received enough money from the sale of my jewelry to take care of the paperwork, purchase an airplane ticket for my mother, and still have a small amount left over. I told Vinh that I expected an exit visa for Mother as soon as possible because I left my husband in Laos by himself and needed to get back there to take care of him.

For two weeks we waited impatiently but heard nothing. My visa would expire in one more week. When Vinh finally appeared at our house at the beginning of the third week, I insisted he take me to see General Hiep. He agreed and drove me to the general's office in Saigon, where we waited about fifteen minutes for the general to arrive.

General Hiep and I shook hands and introduced ourselves. He just kept staring at me without giving me the news I wanted to hear. Finally he said, "If I had known you were so beautiful, I would have had Vinh bring you sooner. Why do you want to go so soon? I would like to invite you out to dinner."

"I am uncomfortable with your invitation. All you have to do is flip your finger and the pretty girls come running, but I am not that kind of girl."

He continued to stare at me for a few minutes longer and then picked up the phone and called someone from the Ministry of the Interior. After he hung up the phone he said, "Your mother will receive her visa tomorrow. Please come back tomorrow afternoon and pick up her passport."

"Thank you." I spoke very softly, and quickly excused myself and left his office.

The general had ordered Vinh to take me back to Bien Hoa. On the return trip, I asked Vinh, "Does the general always act that strange?"

"Never," he said. "He is a very good man. He looks tough from the outside, but he is really a sensitive and caring man."

At home I told my family the good news and all about the general's strange behavior. Minh quietly listened then explained. "You look like the general's wife who died several years ago. General Hiep's father-in-law was the nephew of my grand aunt. This nephew used to take Jeannette and me to the general's mansion once in a while. As soon as someone entered the mansion, the first thing they saw was a large portrait of his wife. You would think you were looking at Yvonne."

Da Lat is one of the most beautiful places in Vietnam. The temperature seldom varies more than four degrees. It constantly stays between sixty-eight and seventy-two degrees. It is the only place in Vietnam where strawberries can be grown year round. Most of the Vietnamese generals built vacation homes there.

I returned to General Hiep's office the following afternoon to pick up Mother's passport. The general asked me for a picture of myself, but I explained that I never give my picture to anyone except my loved ones.

"Will you be coming back to Vietnam again?" he asked.

"Yes," I replied. "I must come back in a few months to renew my French identification card at the French Embassy, because I am still a French citizen."

"Will you let me know when you return?" General Hiep asked.

"Why?" I was just curious to understand his thinking. It appeared to me as if the general was trying to capture me deep inside his eyes.

He held my hands. "I would like to see you again, Yvonne. You look chic in your white skirt and black blouse." He was right. Although I did not wear expensive clothes, I always dressed right for each occasion.

I slowly drew my hands away from his and politely told him, "It is not necessary for you to know when I return to Vietnam."

The next day my uncle and my family took Mother, Chris, and me to the airport. Aunt Maria cried a lot. She was so happy that the three of us would now be together but also sad because she did not know when she would see us again.

The three of us arrived in Savannakhet on December 5, 1972. Charlie and his boss picked us up at the airport. That night we celebrated at a French restaurant. It was good to be with my husband again.

Chapter 9

The Shadow of My Beloved

The maid prepared the spare bedroom for my mother before our arrival, but I rearranged it the way I thought Mother would like it. Every morning I took Mother and Chris to the nearby restaurant to eat breakfast and then to the market. I was so very happy that the three of my closest loved ones and I were all together once again.

On December 20 Charlie brought the mail home like he usually did.

"We got a Christmas card from some general in Vietnam," Charlie said.

I looked at the card and said, "It is from General Hiep."

"Do we know him?" Charlie asked.

"He was the one that helped on Mother's papers," I replied.

The card, written in French, said, "Best wishes to you and your family." I sent him a card in return with the same greeting, thinking this would be the last contact I would have with him. Two weeks later, however, a letter arrived from him addressed to me. He mentioned that he missed me terribly and thought of me often, which made him very happy. He also asked me to buy a sarong (Lao long skirt) and a bottle of Ba Det, anchovy sauce from Savannakhet, and to bring them with me on my next trip to Saigon. At first I did not want to reply, but I thought I should explain to him that he must not continue to write me. I still remembered the way he held my hand and asked me for a picture of myself.

Charlie, Mother, Chris, and I stayed in Savannakhet almost two months. During that time we met a French army commander at one of the director's parties we attended. The commander was well known by both American and Laotian residents of Savannakhet. Joe Gibson, the director, Charlie's big boss, introduced the commander to us.

"Andrè, this is Charlie and Yvonne Combs." He then turned to us and said, "Andrè Vincent, army commander."

"Je suis très content de vous connaitre. Vous êtes très jolie" (I am very glad to meet you. You are very beautiful).

We shook hands while the maid carried a tray of champagne to serve us.

After some conversation Joe Gibson told the commander, "Andre, Yvonne will have to return to Saigon to renew her French I.D. card."

The commander then turned to me and said, "Bring your card to my office. I will handle the matter for you." Fortunately, he did. I wrote to General Hiep that my I.D. card had been renewed, making the trip to Saigon unnecessary. Weeks later, just before we were scheduled to leave for Vientiane, another letter arrived from the general, stating that he did not feel well and was very depressed. Since there was nothing I could do about his current state of health, I thought nothing more about him.

I thought life was temporarily settled for me and my happiness was being fulfilled, but then I saw another problem arising between Charlie and Mother. Charlie gave Mother a dirty look every time he saw her. He even told Mother, "When we go out, you will stay home."

I was standing there with Chris in my arms. My tears just kept pouring as I witnessed the fight between Mother and my husband.

"Charlie, please; Mother, please." It was all I could say.

I could understand both sides. I even put both of them on a scale and asked myself, "If I must choose between them, which one will I choose? My mother brought me into this world. Besides, when Mother is gone I cannot replace her. I have a responsibility to return all the care that she gave me, and I love her so much. On the other hand, Charlie and I exchanged vows before God. We have a responsibility to each other and to our son. I love him very much also."

I realized this was all part of God's creation in man: no matter how we deal with our everyday lives or how complicated our feelings may get, a true and strong love will conquer in the end. I always prayed in the morning when I arose and again in the evening before bedtime. During the day I communicated with God, asking Him to guide me and give me the wisdom to help others and myself. I never hated anyone or even had a bad thought about those who hurt me, intentionally or not. My mind was occupied with good faith and a belief in my abilities and myself. My motto was, "Belief in myself is knowing myself." During the beginning of our domestic problems, Charlie got transferred to Vientiane, Laos.

Our lives in Vientiane were much worse. Life for me seemed like an ongoing nightmare.

In May 1973 Charlie received a letter from Washington, D.C. His tour ended that June, which meant that all of us would be going to the United States—or so I thought.

"We have one month to pack," I told Charlie.

"Yes, when I turn in the papers, the people from the housing department are going to come and pack our household effects."

"I'll tell Mother to get ready with hers."

"Your mother is not coming."

I was shocked. I kept staring at Charlie; my trembling lips could form no words.

"I love you, honey, but your mother cannot come with us to the United States. We have had too many problems. It would ruin our marriage."

As a result, I felt so frustrated that one night I sat in my mother's bedroom, kissed her on her gray hair, and comforted her.

"We should be grateful that we are together and give Charlie credit for letting you live with us. Good night, Mom. I love you and always will. I love Charlie too, and I will take care of both of you till the end of time."

When I walked in my bedroom, I tried to explain to Charlie, "I am sorry that my mother made you uncomfortable. She didn't mean to do that to hurt us."

My husband and I had three days left of our life together in a foreign country. I prayed, *Dear God, no matter what I do, it is not going to be easy for me.* Do I go to the United States with my husband and leave my mother behind alone and uncared-for—a mother who brought me into this world and nurtured me with the last drop of her milk? I could still feel the thought of that on my innocent lips. How could I abandon her and perhaps never see her again? To lose two parents who still remained on this earth, knowing I could neither see them nor touch them again was overwhelming. My emotions were about to drop me in my tracks.

If I returned to Vietnam with Mother, I would be breaking my vow to God and to my husband. I belonged to Charlie and should be with him wherever he went. Then, there was my son Christopher to consider as well. I would not let him grow up without both of us and have him called "half-breed" like his mother.

I could not abandon my mother. "Charlie is stronger than Mother. He can make it," I thought. I decided to go back to Vietnam and take Christopher with me. This would be Charlie's and my last night together. As I began packing Charlie's suitcase I looked out the bedroom window. The dark clouds seemed to be moving very fast. Inside our bedroom, the atmosphere was very heavy. I sat on our bed with a pillow on my chest. Charlie, lying on the bed, looked at me. "Charlie, I will always love you," I told him as our eyes met. My words mixed with my tears. I wanted to tell him many things, but that was all I could say. I had endured the misery and torment far too long not to justify making a severe complaint. That night was the longest night of my life. We held each other all night long without making love, even though it was our last night together.

The next day, June 21, Chris and I took Charlie to the airport. We exchanged our good-bye kisses. "Even though the oceans and mountains are between us, I will always love you," I told Charlie. He started walking extremely fast to the plane. I wanted to run after him and bring him back, but my feet stood helplessly still. My tears fell in the shadow of my departing beloved. Am I singing the same song my mother sang so long ago?

J'attendrai le jour et la nuit!
J'attendrai toujour, ton retour.

I am waiting day and night!
I am waiting every day for your return.

When the plane took off, I stood there holding my son tightly in my arms. Both of us watched the plane fly out of sight and Charlie out of our lives. "Mommy, Daddy goes bye-bye in the *ooh*!" Chris said, his little finger pointing skyward in the direction of the airplane. He could not say "airplane," only "ooh." I then remembered that Charlie had taken Chris to see the airplanes when we lived in Savannakhet; otherwise, Chris refused to go to sleep.

The three of us went back to the house for one more night before catching our flight for Saigon the next morning. At home, I handed Chris to Mother, and I escaped into the bedroom. I noticed the two pillows lying next to each other, touching. One had a familiar smell, but the person who had placed his head on it every night was missing. I picked up the pillow and smelled it. I wanted to smell my husband. With overwhelming grief I remembered that this was the third time I had experienced a departing loved one, not knowing whether I would ever see him again. First Captain Pouley, with the last smell of the French in my motherland of Vietnam, then Ben, and now Charlie! June 21, 1973 was the longest and loneliest night of my life, and I knew I would never forget it. Once more I prayed for strength.

I went out and sat on the porch. Heavy, dark clouds, swollen with rain, were merging with the horizon. With infinite sadness I turned my attention to the palm trees growing by the front porch. The growing wind swept the dust and the branches of the palm trees. As I watched the rain beginning to fall in torrents, I imagined the gloom and chill of separation, of collapse and tragedy. I knew I was hurt. My mind flashed back to the first time I met Charlie in his office.

The admiration that shone in his eyes when he looked at me was still stamped deeply in my mind's eye. My eyes became bathed in a river of tears. It seemed like I met him such a short time ago, yet we became immediate friends. Charlie always made the day brighter when trouble burdened me so. He brought a smile to my innocent lips and then slammed the window to my soul shut. My vanity was deeply wounded by our separation. I could not forget those passing moments we spent together, now indelibly etched for eternity in my mind. They were the only times that we ever really fled the bounds of time and space.

Once again I heard our song, "In the Still of the Night," playing somewhere far off in the distance. I seemed to be living two lives. The shadow of my life is my marriage, while the real life is my happiness, which I somehow never realized. For so long now I have longed to be loved.

Harking back to the trials of my childhood, the war that brought my parents together, and the second war that captured my youth reminded me that both Mother and I were flower buds who didn't have a chance to fully blossom and bloom.

My uncle picked us up the next afternoon in Saigon. I told my family that Charlie had been transferred to Africa and we had to stay with them for a while. Deep in my mind I believed that God would give us the chance to live together again. Charlie and I still wrote to each other, but I never asked him to change his mind about my mother. I didn't want to push him. I missed his so much and worried about him constantly.

Late the next day Vinh came to Bien Hoa to visit my cousin. I asked Vinh to deliver the sarong and anchovy sauce to General Hiep for me. Vinh said, "The general is very sick. He is in the hospital. I would rather you give it to him yourself when he is better." I nodded.

Two days later, Vinh was again in Bien Hoa on military business and stopped by our house. He asked Minh to let him speak to me right away. I had just returned from the market when Vinh saw me. "You won't believe this, but I told the general that you were back, and he was so happy and said, 'My pretty lady is back.' He sent me to ask you to wait a couple of weeks and then bring the sarong and anchovy sauce in person."

I did not give Vinh a definite yes or no, thinking that it was not important at the time.

Every day I was totally consumed with my situation in Vietnam and my husband in the United States. I read one book after another, but it was difficult for me to concentrate on what I was reading. I wrote to my father briefly just to say hello, but never mentioned any of my problems to him.

Something was beginning to tell me that I would soon face another unpleasant situation. A week later Vinh came to our house again and told us, "General Hiep is dead." For a few minutes I just stood there stunned.

"What did he die from?"

"He had cancer. Will you come to the funeral?"

I did not know whether I should.

After giving the matter some thought, I decided it might be appropriate. The day of the funeral I went to Saigon dressed in a white skirt and black blouse, the same clothes I wore the first time I met him. When I arrived I went straight to his casket and looked at his picture placed in front of his casket. I prayed. I really hoped that he would rest in peace. It was the only time I ever called him by his first name, which he had asked me to do many times in his letters. I gently placed the sarong down in front of the casket and handed the anchovy sauce to his sister-in-law. She asked me to spend a few minutes with her, and we went into the next room where she offered me a seat. She then poured a cup of tea for both of us and began telling me about General Hiep.

"He missed you a lot. When he received your last letter, he was so happy that even the people who worked for him got a break. He told me that when you came back to Vietnam, he was going to try every way he could to not let you go away again. Whatever you wanted, he was going to make sure to please you."

Her words shocked me. I had not known that the general was that serious about me. I had only seen him twice. How could he fall in love with me when he didn't know anything about me?

I couldn't figure it out. My last two letters to him had been no more than friendly greetings. I got up and excused myself to leave. She offered to have a chauffeur to drive me back to Bien Hoa. When I arrived home I still could not believe that General Hiep was gone. I never loved him or even considered him a friend because I never got to know him.

Four months had gone by when I received a letter from Charlie asking me to come to the United States and bring my mother. I was so happy, but worried and uncertain about what lay ahead. I went to Saigon and applied for a visa. Mother's exit visa was still good, but she needed an entry visa from the American Embassy. I saw Mr. Han, who worked at the branch of the embassy located in Bien Hoa. He and I were friends, having worked next door to each other at USAID in 1968. Han told me I should go back to the United States with Chris, because Mother's visa would take a while to process. He promised to contact me when her visa was ready.

Mother also told me to plan to leave for the United States, since my visa would expire in a week. I said good-bye to my mother, whom I loved very much. This time, however, I would at least be traveling with my son. Our separation and move to the United States would not be easy for me. Everything would be new—the long journey, living in a new country with a different culture, and the uncertainty of the future.

I was glad to arrive in Kansas City, Missouri, and see my husband again after a six-month separation. I had not even thought of what our home would be like, for we had sent Charlie's mother the money to purchase us a place while we were in Vietnam. She had bought us a handyman's special in Lake of the Ozarks, Missouri. When we arrived at the house that afternoon and I saw it for the first time I had to make an extremely big effort to control myself.

I was shocked. I did not say anything, deciding instead that if this was all we could afford, then this is where we would live. My main concern was that we all be together again.

The house was formerly a bar and restaurant combination, which meant that major remodeling would be necessary. The kitchen located at the rear of the building did not need much alteration, but the large bar room would have to be converted to a living room and two bedrooms. We contracted a local carpenter to do the work. The carpenter also arranged a place for us to stay during the remodeling. We helped the carpenter whenever possible, which reduced his labor costs.

After five weeks the carpenter called to inform us that our house was finished. We were so excited to see what our house would look like. Charlie carried me inside the house and said, "This is a small place, but this is our first home in America, Mrs. Combs."

I was very careful not to get pregnant again. Although I wanted another child, I realized that it would not be right to bring another one into the world because of the age difference between Charlie and me.

"Sweetie, I know it is hard for you here because you have always had a maid before and now you have to do everything yourself," Charlie said sadly.

"Don't worry about the details. I will manage it. That is life! Today we can be riding an elephant, but tomorrow we might be chasing the dog."

Each night I prepared food ahead for the next day so we could devote the full daylight time to working on the house. We spent several days repairing the roof. I sewed all the curtains for the house by hand, carefully measuring each window and piece of fabric so nothing was wasted. Although we needed a new refrigerator, I decided to keep the old one, because we had to save our money for more important things for the house. Charlie, however, insisted on a new refrigerator, informing me that we could get one without paying cash. I was surprised. I had never heard of such a thing—being able to buy something without paying for it at the time of purchase. But Charlie took me to the store the next day and bought a new refrigerator with a plastic card. It was my first encounter with what would become *Mon ami* (My friend)! I soon learned that MasterCard could also be my friendly enemy, especially the day the bill was due.

It took us four months to completely renovate our home. It was so cute, and I was very proud of all our hard work. It was something that we could now call home. As they say, "Houses are made of wood and stone, but only love can make a home." This is where we would begin to raise our family in peace with love and hope for a better tomorrow.

Charlie would go out in the boat most mornings and put a trotline in the river to catch catfish. He loved to fish and hunt. It was the Indian in him. Everything was new to me—the customs, the food, even the countryside. I had no friends. I guess it was because we lived in a retirement community, and I was the youngest there. I kept myself busy remodeling the house and writing to my mother every day and following up with the embassy for my mother's entry visa in order for her to join us in my new country. I was very lonesome because Charlie left early each morning and did not return until sunset.

I got busier and busier cleaning the house, cooking, crocheting, and taking care of Chris. I even cut the grass with a push mower and read and wrote a lot. I did not watch television, though, because I considered it a waste of time to watch those useless daytime shows. I could not understand most of them, as I could not figure out why so many people had so many problems. I did enjoy a few shows like *Bonanza* and *The Andy Griffith Show.* My favorite show was *The Waltons*. I loved their close-knit family, and I always felt like I was one of them. I particularly enjoyed the religious programs relating to our Creator.

I began to be concerned about our budget. Although we could get by on Charlie's retirement pay, I thought that I should plan for my son's college, even if it was a good way off yet. I decided to go to work to supplement our income. Once a week I had to drive twenty miles to town to wash clothes and shop at the grocery store. One time when I was at the grocer I found myself short on money. The clerk told me to write a check. To which I replied, "Ma'am, I am sorry, but I cannot write a check because I am not an American citizen."

"Who on earth told you that?" she asked, looking at me rather puzzled. From her surprised look, I realized something was wrong. I didn't want to tell her that it was Charlie who told me that.

"I just came from another country overseas, and maybe I was given the wrong information," I meekly replied.

"Honey, don't let anyone tell you any crud like that."

"Excuse me," I said softly, "but I don't understand what you are saying. What does *crud* mean?" The clerk smiled and explained the meaning of the word to me in simple Missouri countryside language. I understood. Now I had a slang word to add to my new language.

When I got home from the store, I asked Charlie if I could talk to him for a few minutes. "Is it true that I cannot write a check because I am not yet an American citizen, or is there some other reason?" I asked.

Charlie looked at me with a pained expression. "Sweetie, I had bad experiences with my former wives. They spent more money than I made, but I know you are not like them. I'm very sorry."

I explained to Charlie that if it had not been for the clerk in the store, I probably would never have found out. Instead of getting mad, I told him I understood and that maybe he had the right to feel that way. I just wished that the legal system was such that a man could be judged fairly and not allow a woman to destroy his career and leave him in the doldrums financially when he goes through a divorce. Of course that should work for the woman as well.

I had now been in the United States about eight months, and I missed my mother more and more. I kept praying and waiting for good news from the embassy in Saigon. Then on July 20, 1974, around 11:30 p.m., the phone rang. Mr. Han was calling from Vietnam to tell me that Mother had been granted an entry visa. Mother was standing next to him, waiting her turn to talk to me. My tears flowed with happiness. I told my mother that I would be in Vietnam within a week to bring her to the United States.

I would need enough money to buy airplane tickets for my mother, Chris, and myself. *Mon amie!* My friendly enemy, MasterCard, rescued me. "Boy!" I thought. "Could I ever make a commercial for MasterCard!"

It was time to say good-bye once again. This time I told Charlie our separation would not be as long as before. I would return as soon as possible. Charlie took Chris and me to the Kansas City airport, and our flight departed for Vietnam late in the afternoon. We stopped in Los Angeles for a six-hour layover that night before we could get another flight to Hawaii. From there I took China Airlines and had to check out of one building and catch a bus to another building for the international flight. I had purchased plenty of baby food and milk, which I carried in one hand while carrying Chris in the other. I could not check in because it was too early. I sat in a chair, trying to feed Chris, a bit scared to be by myself at that time of the morning. I thought of my love for Mother, and that gave me new courage. A couple of hours later an elderly woman came over and we talked. I felt more comfortable.

"Hi. Where are you going?" she asked.

"I'm going to Saigon," I replied.

"I'm going to Hawaii to see my daughter. Does this flight go direct to Saigon or do you have to change flights?"

"They will stop in Hawaii and then on to Taipei. I have an overnight layover and flight change the next day to Saigon."

"It must be difficult for you to travel by yourself with a little boy. He is cute."

"Thank you."

When we arrived and had greeted my mother after so long an absence, I became concerned because she did not look well. She told me how much she had missed us. I tried to console her and determined that there was no way I was going back without her. We would never be separated again. I also explained to her that I had brought some extra money just in case we needed it for any other papers for her to leave the country.

"Where did you get the money?" she asked.

"I sold my diamond watch, some ivory that I had bought before, a typewriter, and our black lacquer room divider."

She broke into tears. "I remember the time you brought me to Laos you had to sell your diamond rings, including your engagement ring. This time it is the rest of your jewelry and part of your household items."

I wiped the tears from her face and told her, "Mom, please don't feel bad. You are the most important person in my life. Material things can be replaced. I cannot replace you. Our love, health, happiness, and freedom are important. Money and material things are simply transactions from one hand to another."

The next morning I went to see Han and told him how much I appreciated all he had done for me. The following day I went to the Ministry of the Interior in Saigon to renew her exit visa so she would be ready to travel. They had canceled her exit visa! She had not used it the last time, because she didn't have an entry visa. I returned to Bien Hoa and told my family the bad news. I said nothing after that, not wanting to make my mother feel guilty or hopeless. Once again I had decided that almost anything could be done with faith, strength, an ability to cope, and a willingness to work a problem out.

I took a long walk along the Dong Nai River. I just wanted to communicate with God without anything interfering with my thoughts. I had sometimes taken walks like this before when my difficult problems seemed insurmountable. My prayers and my faith had always given me the insight and ability to solve a particularly difficult problem when the solution seemed impossible. I returned home and still said nothing more to my family. They worried about me. They had never seen me looking so strange and being so quiet. I took a cold shower, washed my hair, and went to bed with an empty stomach. I had begun that night to cleanse my spirit with a clean diet. I did not eat anything with blood, such as beef, chicken, pork, or fish. All I had was fruit, bread, rice, and spinach for four months.

Time was getting more critical with each passing day. In just ten more days, my visa was going to expire and I would have to leave for the United States again without my mother unless I could get her visa squared away. With an idea forming in my mind, I asked Jeannette to rub some soap on my hand so my jade bracelet would come off. It was the last piece of jewelry I owned, and I was out of money. I knew it would take all the money I could lay my hands on to bribe Vietnamese officials to release my mother's visa. Three more days passed. I now had only one week left. My faith held steady. I decided that I would not leave without Mother, and I was not going to be separated from my husband ever again.

That afternoon as I sat by a tree in the backyard deep in thought, I noticed the maid nearby reading a magazine. I looked at her with joy. I remembered the time I first taught her how to read, the time I had given her my savings so she could buy clothes to wear when she went back to her village for Tet (the Vietnamese New Year). I had always cared for my servants, and I never looked down on them.

"Miss Yvonne, do they have many different colors of cars in the United States?" she asked.

"Yes, they do."

"What color do you think is the prettiest?"

I replied, "I like white, because I think it is a touch of class."

"I like blue." She continued to read without further comment.

Blue. I finally got up and went into the house to find my mother. "I'm going to the market for a couple of hours," I informed her. Mother was surprised, but thought I probably needed something.

Instead of the market, however, I visited Lan, one of my high school roommates. She had dropped out of school to become a bargirl. During her work around the bar, she had met an American named Tom. Tom had the reputation of being the biggest bum in Vietnam. According to Lan, every time Tom came into the bar, he would announce that he had just slept with all the girls in Vietnam. Lan would tease, "Except one."

"You just arrange the meeting," Tom would tell her. "I will pay whatever the price it takes. You know me. I'm just a good ol' sugar daddy."

"No, you can't, because she is not one of us. She is very special. She is a métisse."

"What is a métisse?"

Lan explained, "She's half French and half Vietnamese and has big breasts. What could be a better combination? These women are beautiful." Tom told Lan to arrange a meeting with me for him and he would pay her.

That is why I went to see Lan. I knew Tom was crazy about wanting me. The thought had come to my mind when the maid said she liked a blue car. Tom owned a blue sports car. I also knew that Tom, the bum, would not help me unless he got something in return. I had already decided to willingly sell my body in order to get enough money for my mother's visa. I felt I had no choice.

I knocked on Lan's door. She was very surprised to see me. She didn't know what to say. "Is Tom still in Vietnam?" I asked.

"Yes, but only for two more days." Her reply made me nervous. I asked her if she could get in touch with him. She said she would try but could not promise. Then she looked at me and laughed, "I can't believe what you just said. I always thought—" Lan stopped short of what she wanted to say. "OK, I will try to arrange a meeting for you because Tom would give me a big tip for this."

I looked the other way, knowing she was happy about my request because she thought that she could drag me down to her level. I did not care what she thought of me because I knew I was going to do whatever I had to do in order to get my mother out of Vietnam. I did not want her condolence or sympathy. I told Lan good-bye and left. I went home with a very heavy heart.

About 10:30 the next morning, Lan drove her moped to my house. The maid came in and called me. Lan gave me Tom's address in Saigon and told me to be there by 1:00 p.m. Tom would be waiting. I explained to my mother and family that I had to go to Saigon. Lan knew someone there that might help me with the visa.

When I arrived in Saigon I had a difficult time finding Tom's place. Finally I found the right house and knocked on the door. A handsome young man in his thirties opened the door.

"Are you Tom?" I asked.

"Come in," he said.

My heart was beating too fast, my feet felt like ice, and my face felt hot. I was very nervous, like a person on trial waiting for the judge to announce the sentence. "Sit down on the bed," he said. He sat next to me and lit a cigarette. He held the cigarette in one hand, while touching my shoulder with the other. I began shaking all over.

"May I please use your bathroom?" I asked. He pointed, and I walked in that direction. Once inside the bathroom, I shut the door. Leaning against the wall, I closed my eyes and prayed "Dear God, please forgive me. My body will not be clean after this day, but my soul is yours. Today I ate only rice, fruit, and spinach. I commit my clean spirit and all my faith to You." Then, turning my thoughts to my family, I pleaded, "Mother, Charlie, and Chris, please forgive me for what I am about to do because of the love I have for my mother."

I walked out of the bathroom like a new person. I was not afraid anymore. I went back and sat on the bed next to Tom, my blouse still partly open. He lit up another cigarette and ran his fingers through my thick, long hair. I sat as still as a statue. Tom reached under the bed and pulled out a paper bag and handed it to me. At first, I thought it was a bag of clothes.

"Take it and pay those leeches. Just make sure you get a visa for your mother before you give them the money."

Tom gave me one hundred twenty thousand piasters, equal to four hundred dollars. I looked at him, my eyes wide. "How did you know I needed money for my mother's visa?"

"Lan told me. Lan's a bad girl. She was thrilled that I'd get the chance to sleep with the last Vietnamese girl. But she was wrong, because I shall leave the last one alone to be part of my memories of my tour of duty in Vietnam. I realize that you are somebody that I'd like to remember with respect for the rest of my life."

My emotions overwhelmed me. I could not believe what I had just heard. I broke down and cried. Tom held both my hands and said, "After you get the visa, leave as soon as you can. I wish you and your mother a safe trip and good luck in America. This is a small world, so we may see each other again someday. Lan told me that you were the best in school in literature and essays. If you should write a book someday, don't forget this. I will always remember you as a beautiful person. I think you should go now. I'm leaving tomorrow."

"I really appreciate the help. Bon voyage to you too." We gave each other a long hug. It was the beginning of a friendship that I had not planned. Tom gave me a kiss on my forehead. His eyes were red, and I realized he had been crying a little bit. We finally said good-bye to each other, and he waved at me as I walked out of the house and repeated once more, "Good luck in America!"

As I caught the bus back to Bien Hoa, all I could think of was the fact that Mother, Chris, and I would soon be reunited with Charlie. I couldn't stop thinking about Tom and what a decent man he turned out to be after all. Then I remembered the maid telling me she liked a blue car, which was what Tom had. Was this the way God had fulfilled my faith? At home, I told my family that I might get Mother's visa soon. I did not go into detail about Tom or the money. Until now, Mother did not know where the help came from.

The next day I took the money and paid all the officials necessary to obtain the visa. I had only six days left. The officials told me to return at about 5:00 that afternoon and the visa would be ready. I walked out of the building and noticed Mother and Chris sitting under a distant tree waiting for me. As I walked toward them I thought that the weather was hot, even for December.

We stopped at a little sandwich shop along the sidewalk.

"Mom, what would you like?" I asked.

"A ham sandwich and a lemonade," she said.

I ordered the two sandwiches and two lemonades. I wet the napkin to wipe my mother's face and told her, "Everything is going to be all right, Mom. We will get the visa this time."

"I hope so," she said.

I then held Chris so Mother could rest.

We waited until 5:00. When I returned to the office my mother's visa had been stamped on the passport. I took a deep breath and released a sigh of relief. The official handed the passport to me but did not turn it loose. He kept looking at my watch and my white gold chain. Even though I had paid them earlier in the day, it became obvious that he wanted whatever I had left. Taking off my watch and chain, I handed them to him. I kept the crucifix, the small charm that was on the chain, however, because it meant so much to me.

I ran out of the offices of the Ministry of the Interior to my mother and showed her the passport with the visa. "My daughter, are you sure we have it this time?" I knew she was worried about everything coming through at the last minute. Anything could happen in Vietnam at the last minute. I took Mother and Chris, and we rushed to the airline office. The earliest day we could leave would be five days from now, and my visa expired in six.

When we got home Mother told the rest of the family the good news. I took a shower, prayed, and jumped into bed. The next day I took a long walk, taking my last look at Bien Hoa, where I was born and raised. I walked by Ma Soeur's school, the middle school, my old high school, and then on down to the

Dong Nai River. Before returning home I bought a sardine sandwich along the sidewalk and walked to the Virgin Mary statue. I stood there and looked at my secret place where I used to come and where I first found God's protection. I felt like I was home. I knelt down and thanked God that I had fulfilled my faith in Him and that He must have been pleased with me. I broke my diet that day after forty days of bread, rice, fruit, and spinach. I decided to eat my sardine sandwich there. My tears were mixed with my food and my voice as I prayed aloud, "Lord Jesus, when I was six years old, I came here every morning to hide and eat my sandwich. At that time I didn't know how to pray. I only knew how to call upon Your name. Lord Jesus, please protect me. This will probably be the last time I come here, but I know You will be with me wherever I am, to the end of time."

Finally I went to pay respect to my ancestors for the last time.

When I returned home it was almost 7:00 p.m. I stood by my gate and looked up at the two-story next door where Ben used to live. This gate had not been knocked on for seven years and two months by "Mr. Blue Eyes." I wished that it could be knocked on once more for the "English for Today" lesson.

Jeannette loaned me fifty dollars for spending money to get me back to the United States. We left on Christmas Day in 1974. I took one last look at Vietnam and quickly thought about its two thousand years of history. Then I closed my eyes and once more thanked God for everything. At least my son would not grow up in Vietnam. In America he would not have to suffer with the title of "métisse." Instead of a life of sorrow, he would be able to have a McDonald's Big Mac whenever he wished. I could feel the warm tears on my cheeks. This time, however, these were tears of happiness and promise.

We ate dinner on the plane. Because Mother was taking a special medication, I realized that she would soon be hungry again, so I wrapped up my steak and a piece of bread and kept a Seven Up. I put the package in my handbag for her when she wanted them.

We flew the same route back to the United States as I did going to Vietnam. The plane arrived in Taipei that evening, and we checked into a hotel for the night. I was more relaxed this time because I finally had my mother with me again. About midnight, Mother awakened hungry. Smiling, I took the steak, bread, and drink from my handbag and handed them to her.

"I can't believe how much you love and care for me," she said.

"I will always love you, Mom." I turned over and went to sleep.

We spent Christmas Day on the plane. I thought about Charlie and could hardly wait to see him. Then I remembered we would gain a day coming back because of our crossing the International Date Line going eastward. That meant we would arrive in the United States on Christmas Day.

We left the hotel in Taipei for the airport a little early. When we arrived, we walked around and shopped with the fifty dollars Jeannette loaned me. I bought Mother a sweater for Christmas, Chris a little airplane, and my husband a pipe, leaving me with fifty-seven cents in change. I kept the fifty-seven cents, which I still have to this day, to remind me that most good things in life come through struggling. After we boarded the plane and settled down comfortably in our seats, I looked at the coins again, smiled, and remembered, "God told me that the number 57 would have considerable meaning later in my life."

I became ecstatic that I had made the trip and accomplished so much. As I fell into a deep sleep, I started dreaming of being with Charlie again. After a brief stop in Hawaii we continued on to Los Angeles, arriving there on Christmas morning U.S. time. Looking at my wrist to check the time, I suddenly remembered that I no longer owned a watch. It had gone to the Vietnamese official as part of the deal for Mother's visa.

Charlie met us at the airport in Kansas City with the most pleasant expression on his face. I told him that we would never be separated again and that whatever problems should arise we would work them out together.

On April 29,1975, only four months after we left, South Vietnam fell to the communists. Sometimes I think of how close we came to not making it out. What would have happened to us if we had tried to leave one day later, when my visa expired?

Mother and I in 1950

This picture was taken just before Mother and I took Captain Pouley to board his ship back to France.

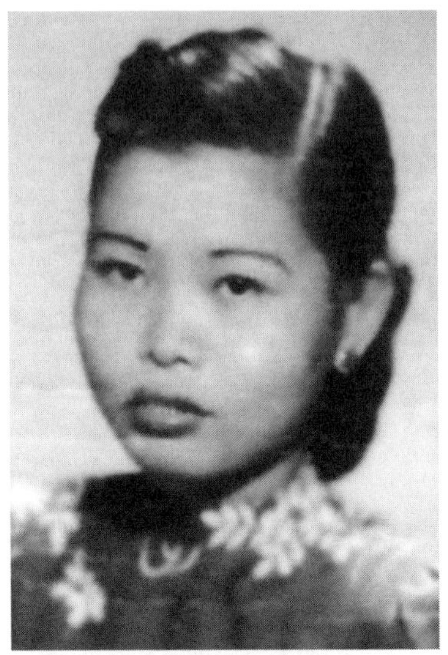

This is a picture of my mother taken in 1954. Mother was twenty-seven years old.

This is the photo my sister found in our father's office. I was three years old.

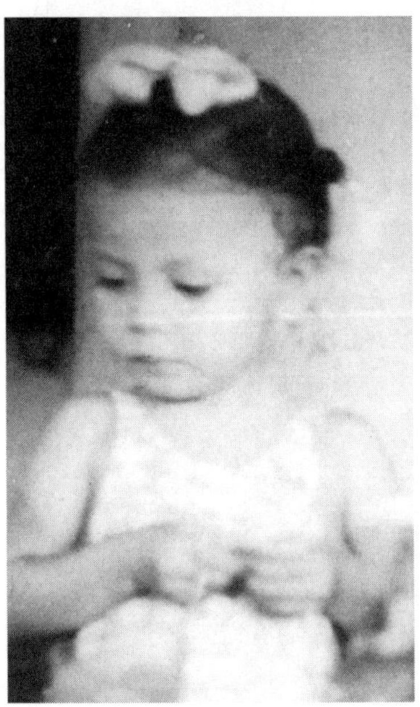

1951 when my father came back to Vietnam to take me to France

This is the last time I smiled before I faced the hardships of life. I was five years old.

1951 when my father came back to Vietnam to take me to France

This is where I lived in Bien Hoa Airbase

I saved one piastre each day for 320 days to purchase my first pilot pen.

Flood in Vietnam

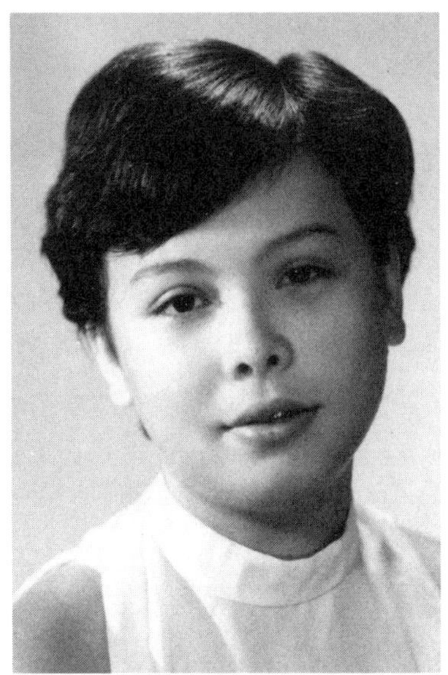

This picture of me was taken at the age of twenty-four.

This picture of me was taken at the age of thirty-nine.

Our wedding day, March 16, 1970

Chris and I in 1973

Chris at the age of eight playing Little League

My beloved son Chris at the age of sixteen

Chris with Grandmother, 1992

Chris in Korea, 1991

Headstone on Chris's grave

On top of the Matterhorn, 1995

Switzerland, 1995

Perouge, 1995

Restaurant in Zermatt

With Charlie at Busch Gardens

This is the cake decorated with thirty-six poinsettias representing Mother's thirty-six days of faith (December 1999).

I visited this place when I returned to Vietnam in 2001. This is where I used to hide and found God's protection at the age of six.

My prayer room

Vietnam, 2001

Chapter 10

The Pursuit of Happiness

Finally we were together and very happy for a while. I told Charlie, "I appreciate it very much that you let Mother come."

"I know how much you love your mother and worried about her and wanted to take care of her. That was one of the reasons I fell in love with you. Throughout my traveling life, I have seen some women whose good times come first. It aggravated them to help their sick, bedridden parents—to fix a bowl of soup or watch them for a day or two."

"There are some good women out there," I said. "They always call and check on their parents, even though they have to work, come home and cook, and take care of kids. To me, parents are to be loved, not to be left behind."

"Let's walk down to the river to see what kind of fish they caught today," Charlie said.

"I'll go get Chris and then we'll go," I said.

The three of us walked down to the river just a few feet from our house. I turned my head around and said to Charlie, "Look, our house is so cute. I'm happy with it, simply because we've remodeled most of it ourselves."

"I like it too. I'm glad that the big project is over. Now I can go fishing."

"Do you need a boat to go fishing?"

"I do. In the meantime I can go with Henry on his boat. He invited me to go with him to put the trotline in the river."

From that day, Charlie began his new adventure—fishing. Charlie even fished when the snow was deep on the ground. Chris used to get a kick out of it when he slid down the hill with his snowsuit to bring his daddy a coffee bottle. Chris was three-and-a-half at the time.

Once a week I went to the store. I shopped very carefully, often right down to the penny, and made sure Mother, Charlie, and Chris had good, nutritious meals.

After a few months Charlie became concerned about our health care. He told me, "Since I am retired from the military, we should move closer to the military base so we can benefit from the medical care and other benefits we are eligible for."

"Sounds like we don't have much choice," I said. I agreed to move even though I didn't want to leave our home.

We bought another home in Waynesville, Missouri, which was four miles to Fort Leonard Wood Army Base. Charlie landed a job shortly after that.

Three months after our move to Waynesville, disaster struck again. I was baking a macaroni casserole in the oven one afternoon when the oven blew up as I turned on the oven light to check the dinner. Flames engulfed the house. I helped Mother and Chris out of the house and then went back inside to retrieve the suitcase with all our important papers. I turned the dog loose and then closed the valve on the gas tank outside. I called the fire department from our next-door neighbor's house, but by the time the truck arrived, the place was destroyed. The three of us sat out in the yard until sunset, patiently waiting for Charlie to come home from work. Mother cried over and over again, "My

God, why can't my daughter get a break. One thing happens to her after another." Somehow, I remained calm.

Charlie's boss and his family took us all into their home and cared for us for ten days. Bless their hearts. I will always remember them for their Christian charity.

As a result of the fire we moved back to our first home in Warsaw. I tried to salvage some of my dishes, which were badly damaged from the smoke and required a lot of time and elbow grease to clean. I told Charlie that I was serious about working. While riding around one day, we found a hamburger drive-in, complete with ice cream and milkshake equipment. I wanted to buy that business, but in order to do so, we would have had to sell our house. Fortunately, our house sold in six weeks and we bought the business. The drive-in was located on Highway 65, about fifty miles from Springfield and five miles from Lake of Pomme De Terre.

During the two years we owned the restaurant, business flourished. It was very hard work though. One day Charlie announced that he was tired of making banana splits and Coney Island hotdogs. He wanted to move to Florida to retire and go saltwater fishing. "Look in the United Farm Catalog and Strout Realty Magazine to see if there is a place you might enjoy," I told him.

The restaurant demanded my constant attention from seven in the morning until eleven at night every day of the week. After we closed at night, we would still have to clean all the ice cream machines, scrub the grill and deep fat fryers, and mop the floors.

Each day Charlie grew more and more restless, wanting to move to Florida. Finally he began insisting that we sell the business. Even though I was skeptical, I had to consider Charlie's side. He had spent his career in the military and had been a prisoner of the Japanese in Japan from 1941 to 1945. The time had come for Charlie to begin enjoying life, and I thought I should do whatever I could to make him happy. I loved my husband and wanted him to live a happy life for whatever time he had left. So I agreed. Shortly thereafter, on July 19, 1977, we sold our business and moved to Florida.

Our first stop inside Florida was the little town of Crystal River. Later that afternoon we checked into "Nichols Motel," located on the south end of town. Then we went looking for a restaurant for dinner. Driving around the area the next day, Charlie liked what he saw enough to stay, if he could find a nice place on the water. We immediately found a place in Ozello, just south of Crystal River. The real estate lady who had helped us was attentive and observant.

"How do you like the real estate business?" I asked, trying to make conversation.

"It's fun," she replied.

I told her that I enjoyed buying and selling, so the part of the business concerning helping people with their home needs appealed to me. I could see another challenging career for myself. Not only would I match people with their needs but I would also work in a new business. The lady told me about several new real estate courses that would begin in September. I thanked her and decided to check into it. A few days later I went to Inverness, as she had directed, and applied for the course.

At first I did not know my way around from Ozello to Inverness, but with determination I soon mastered the roads as if I had been a long-time resident. While Charlie went fishing, I went to school.

On my first night of school in America, class finished at 9:30 p.m., and I left immediately because I had more than a forty-mile drive back to Ozello.

"How was school?" Charlie asked as I walked in the door.

"Fine. I like it."

"Good. I think you'll enjoy the real estate business."

"I think so too."

After checking on Mother I noiselessly crept into Chris's room. I covered him up and sat down next to his bed, watching him deep in sleep. Many thoughts passed through my mind. I fought the urge to pick him up out of his warm, cozy bed to hold him and kiss him and reassure him that he had nothing to worry about.

Chris was now seven years old and had reached the stage where he began to worry about his parents' circumstances. He didn't quite understand why Mommy worked all the time and Mommy and Daddy no longer slept in the same bed together. Looking at that sweet, innocent face, I determined at once that I would use all my powers that God had given to me to keep my family together, whatever the tragedy in life might be, simply because I loved my husband. My son needed and deserved both parents. Today we still remain under one roof.

Since it was a little cool that night, I checked Charlie's bedroom to see if he had a blanket. We had not slept together or made love for over two years because of his impotence, which I had accepted. He was my husband, the father of my child, and I loved him enough just for that. There were many times I wished that I could hold Charlie in my arms, kiss him, make love to him even in the daytime.

Charlie had additional health problems due to the fact that he had been a prisoner of war for forty-five months. Days passed into weeks, months, and then years, until Charlie got old. The bedroom story seemed to close for us; but despite all the sadness, trials, and tribulations, I was so happy that when I woke up in the morning, I brought Charlie a cup of coffee to his bed and said, "Good morning, Mr. Combs." This was the way we started out back in 1968—Mr. Combs and his coffee.

I was glad when I saw Charlie well enough to go fishing or go into the woods hunting. He could not stand the inactivity, especially in dark rooms. Being a prisoner of World War II had some bad effects on him.

I thought about Mother. The Vietnam War had some bad effects on her also. She told me when she was seventeen that she used to hide under the basement full of dirt, holding her breath, watching the Japanese walk by with their bayonets in their hands. Then came the Viet Cong after that. That's why I never considered letting Mother live by herself. She was too afraid she might die. Most of all, I wanted to take care of Mother. I was strong enough to make it, even though I was trapped between loyalties with my situation; but I was so grateful that I still had the chance to bring Charlie a cup of coffee in the morning and Mother a glass of water at night for her medicine.

I knew I had the ability to control myself. During the day, I worked to forget my pain, and at night, I read or wrote. The more I hurt, the better I could write. I was very lonely. Again I prayed for strength.

I passed the real estate exam in 1978. I had put my best into it because the English language was still difficult for me. We sold our house in Ozello and moved to Crystal River. I continued to work in real estate.

In September 1980 I had the opportunity to purchase a Chinese restaurant in Crystal River for a very reasonable price. I briefly described the matter with Charlie, explaining that I could take my two-and-one-half carat diamond ring to the bank for a loan. Charlie had bought me that ring for my twenty-eighth birthday when we owned the business in Missouri. He told me that he trusted my judgment, for which I promptly thanked him.

Fortunately the bank loaned me enough money based on the appraisal of my ring. I bought the business. The previous owner had not done well financially, so he made no improvements to the building.

The first thing I had to do was replace the linoleum in the kitchen. I installed the flooring myself, carefully measuring and then cutting it outside. When I started to carry it inside, however, I realized just how heavy and complicated laying the linoleum can be. I managed to do it anyway. After that was done, I painted the entire restaurant, not quitting until 2:00 a.m. In order for me to save enough money to buy the necessary equipment and inventory, I had to do all the work myself. My routine workday was 7:00 a.m. until midnight, seven days a week.

Luckily I found a Chinese cook who was originally from Taiwan and living in Crystal River. His wife and sister worked as waitresses. Two weeks later the Crystal Pagoda opened its doors, the first Chinese restaurant in Citrus County. The place was always packed at lunchtime, and I am thankful to everyone who brought their business my way.

Although I was very busy with the restaurant, I always went home for one hour each evening to check on my family, especially my son. I would check his homework, read him a short story, and tuck him in before returning to the restaurant.

Since the restaurant was thriving, the chef demanded more money. At first I agreed, but then he demanded even more. I told him, "You and your family have made more money working in my restaurant than you have ever made before. I am the owner, but I only receive a small salary."

"I quit now!" he shouted.

"Very well. You know where the door is."

He said, "You are going to have to close your restaurant if I leave, because you don't know what sauce goes with what food."

The chef was wrong. All my life I kept telling myself, "Be prepared just in case." He did not know that I had quietly tiptoed into the kitchen to watch him while he was cooking. Since I already was a good cook, it didn't take me long to catch on to the secret sauce.

Thursday morning I started to cook. Mother helped me fry the egg rolls and chicken wings. Since I had no waitresses, a buffet was prepared for the lunch crowd. This wouldn't be too difficult.

The most difficult part was trying to stir the huge wok of fried rice. My hands were not made for that kind of work. Being a restaurant staff of one and spending many hours on my feet each day caused my legs to swell by evening.

Four days later I found another chef. He was good. I still had no waitresses and had to wait on tables myself for another five weeks before I found another pair. I used my tip money to buy medicine and other essential items to send to my family in Vietnam, who were most in need. I also sent them the money so that they could buy another essential—food. I would roll a one hundred dollar bill real tight and stuff it into a drinking straw. Then I would seal the ends of the straw with a lighter, and I would insert the straw into a tube of toothpaste.

I had also learned that after the fall of Saigon, my uncle, who had been a commander in the South Vietnamese navy, had been captured and sent to what the North Vietnamese called a "re-education camp." He remained there for nine years.

I further realized that my family was in dire need as victims of the war. Our middle-class family in Vietnam had been torn apart. Like many others there, they had to do whatever was necessary in order to survive in times of war. A bowl of rice, hot or cold, each day was a blessing. No one knew what tomorrow would bring. I continued to operate the restaurant for a couple of years. When the first opportunity presented itself, I decided to sell the business because I never had enough time for my family.

It seemed only a short time long ago that my son was one month old. I used to cradle him in my arms like my mother did when I was a baby. Then he started to walk, talk, and smile. When I picked him up from school, I took him to Karate class or Boy Scouts. I kept all the things he made in class—the pictures he drew or a little note that said, "I love you, Mommy." I still remember how one Mother's Day he picked the flowers along the road and put them in the cooking pot and arranged them into a bouquet of flowers and gave it to me. He was nine years old at the time.

From time to time our family would go to the movies. I liked certain movies or kinds of movies more than others. I especially enjoyed love stories, musicals, and inspirational stories with a moral, educational theme. They still leave me feeling terrific afterwards. Perhaps my all-time favorite movie is *Love Story*, primarily because it is about two people and their emotions, trials, and tribulations. For most of us, love is the strongest influence in our lives. A movie about love is entertaining and educational in that we see how others cope with the many problems of life and resolve them through the strength of love. Perhaps it reinforces the love in our own lives.

Inspirational movies help me to see people more in perspective as a whole. Justice somehow triumphs in the end.

I think we need more movies of this nature, for I cannot help but think that most people are influenced in varying degrees by such moral and inspirational movies.

Musicals also play an important role in our lives. The scenery enhances the music, because we all at some time or another dream of getting away from it all.

Chapter 11

THE LAND OF THE MORNING CALM

In 1990 Chris joined the army. I decided that it was the ideal time to begin my book. The house was quiet, and I could concentrate. Since I was eight years old my dream has been to become a famous author. Although I had devoted most of my life to my family, I also owed a great deal to myself. Therefore, I was determined to write my memoirs.

Chris graduated from high school in 1989 and enlisted in the United States Army the following year. After completing basic training at Fort Eustis, he received orders to serve a tour of duty in Korea. While overseas, he called home faithfully once a week to keep us informed about how he was doing. From his calls Chris seemed to be having a good time.

Before our son left for Korea, I wrote him a note telling him everything he should do, should not do, and needed to be aware of.

> Go with your buddies; be careful of your billfold. Be aware of what is going on around you. Refuse if friends try to talk you into something you should not do. Do not get drunk. There are social drinks and also trouble drinks. Do not buy anything from the PX to sell. Don't borrow money or gamble. You never did before; don't start now.

Do not exchange American money at the black market: people see, people talk, people get you in trouble. Let's talk a little bit about girls. These girls can be found at the bar, club, or massage parlor. You probably will go to the bar and here comes a girl who wants to sit with you, talk to you, and then she will ask you for a drink. The longer she sits with you, the more drinks she has to have. The money of these drinks will be split with the bar owner. When the girls sit with you or go to bed with you tonight, it doesn't mean she belongs to you. She might do the same thing with your dear friends or somebody else tomorrow. Do not get mad or fight over that. You'll just get yourself in trouble with the army, friends, and the bar's owner. About massage girls, you probably want just a massage after a long day of work, but the girls might encourage you for something else. In order for the girls to quit working at the bar, their boyfriends must settle their debts with the bar's owner.

There are a lot of tricks from girls. Some girls might inform their boyfriends that they are pregnant. They claim they need the money for an abortion or that their boyfriends have to marry them. In some cases, they are not pregnant. They just want a free ticket to the U.S.

Be extra careful with the little boys in the streets. They might look cute and innocent and say that they just want a piece of chewing gum or chocolate, but they will steal your watch or billfold or take you to see their sisters. VD is a bad disease. It is at the top of the list like AIDS. If you get this, you have to stay in the hospital until you are cured and it goes on your records.

Good luck, son. I wish you a safe tour of duty in the Far East.

Two months after arriving in Korea, Chris called us as usual and casually mentioned that he had met Sujin, a Korean girl who he liked very much and would probably marry one day. Being a mother, I was concerned for both of them.

"Chris is too young," I thought. "After all, he is only nineteen years old. He must first start a career, achieve some of his goals, and obtain some financial security so he can better plan his future." All I could do was wait and see if the relationship between my son and this Korean girl developed any further.

A few months later Chris called and asked me to come to Korea. He needed my help to get all the necessary paperwork finished so he could marry Sujin. Charlie and I were shocked at the news, but gradually we came to the conclusion that no matter how good the advice we gave Chris, based on our own experience, it might not be right for him. "Yvonne," Charlie said, "you have done enough for him. Work on your book. He can handle his own affair."

Charlie was right, but Chris kept calling and begging me to come to Korea and help him. Finally, my resistance worn down, I agreed to fly to Korea. Charlie wanted to come along. Since I could not leave my mother all alone, I decided to hire a close friend of Mother's to stay with her while we were gone.

With that, Charlie and I left for Korea, arriving in Seoul at 10:30 p.m. on a freezing winter's night in January 1991. I was concerned that Charlie might not be able to tolerate such cold weather. Chris met us at the airport with his intended bride. After giving both his parents a big hug, he introduced us to Sujin. Chris said, "Mom and Dad, this is Sujin."

"It is nice to meet you, Sujin," Charlie and I said.

"An yung ya sal," (How are you) Sujin greeted?

Chris helped us with our suitcases, and we headed for the exit. "Since it is so late, why don't we stay here in Seoul tonight?"

Chris suggested. We agreed and rented two rooms. This was my first night in the "Land of the Morning Calm."

The next morning after breakfast we hired a taxi and headed for Wonju. The taxi driver dropped us off on a narrow road in front of a beautiful house that Sujin was renting. The large front gate even had an intercom.

My first impression of Sujin was favorable. Although she spoke very little English, I tried very hard to let her know that I was a very open-minded and understanding person. That way she could relax and be more comfortable with me. Sujin prepared all the meals herself—Korean meals. In the evenings Chris would join us with several of his army buddies from Camp Eagle for dinner.

A Korean man came to the house with all the marriage documents. Some of them Sujin would have to take to Seoul for signatures. When I offered to go with her, the man spoke in a low tone, a half smile on his face. "Don't worry, Mrs. Combs. This is Sujin's country. She knows where to go." I turned toward Sujin and asked if she could go by herself.

"Yes, Mom," she replied.

Chris's tour of duty ended June 6, and we did not want to leave Sujin behind to travel to the United States at a later date by herself. The paperwork took longer than expected. This was frustrating, but for Charlie's sake I could not let it show in front of him. Charlie trusted me and went along with me about everything, believing that there was no problem that I could not solve. I always said, "I'll take care of it," and I usually did.

The first time I spoke those words, I was eight years old. My cousin Jeannette and I wanted to see our favorite Indian movie so badly but had no money. Jeannette kept asking me, "Yvonne, what are we going to do?"

"I'll take care of it," I heard myself say once again when Chris and Sujin came to me, worried because June 6 was only one week away and Chris would be leaving. Fortunately, the Korean man dropped off Sujin's passport and other important papers just four days before we were scheduled to leave. I suggested to Sujin that she visit her sister in Kannung to pay her final respects to her ancestors before she left with us, just like I did when I left Vietnam. The next morning we got up very early to catch the bus from Wonju to Kannung. The three-hour trip was the roughest bus ride I had ever taken.

When we arrived at her sister's house, I thought I had reached the end of the Land of the Morning Calm. Sujin's sister and brother-in-law greeted us at the door. They were kind to us and seemed to be very nice people—hard-working people—which greatly impressed me. They gave Charlie and me their bedroom for the one night we stayed with them. Charlie was so tired from the trip that he fell into a deep sleep as soon as his head touched the pillow.

"Tonight is the last evening Sujin will spend with her sister. It will be a long time before they see one another again," I thought. Sujin would be going to a new country without any knowledge of the customs, language, or food. With no friends or family, she would be alone. Foreigners all think that America has everything, America is heaven on earth, and when they get to America they will be well taken care of. What they often do not realize is that people in the West also have to work hard to achieve their goals in life. Our quality of life all depends on each and every one of us and our capabilities and desires to succeed. To me, America is a promised land with doors of opportunity open for anyone that wants it bad enough to carry their potential to the fullest.

I must have finally fallen asleep. I heard soft voices coming from the kitchen. When I opened my eyes I realized it was morning, and Sujin's sister was apparently preparing breakfast for us. I turned over and shook Charlie awake. "Mr. Combs, who is making coffee this morning?" I kidded him.

"Well..." he began. I looked at him with a smile, knowing exactly what his reply meant. We both got out of bed, dressed quickly, and walked a few steps out into the living room. Sujin's sister greeted us warmly in Korean, with Sujin acting as our interpreter. "Good morning. Your breakfast is ready."

I noticed that her sister had prepared rice, kimchi (a salty salad consisting of cabbage, red pepper, garlic, ginger, green onions), another vegetable, and coffee for us. I looked at Charlie, concerned that my husband might not be able to eat the rice and kimchi. In a low voice, I said, "Charlie, try to eat a little bit and wash it down with the coffee. You will be all right."

As we were all sitting on the floor around the table and eating, Sujin addressed me. "Mom, my sister is going to come back to Wonju with us and stay for three days until we leave."

"That's wonderful," I replied.

After breakfast we caught the bus back to Wonju. During those three days we left Sujin and her sister to visit one another while Charlie and I went to Seoul and Osan.

When we got back to Sujin's house, I helped her pack all her household items. She showed me a Korean costume that her sister had bought for her. "Try it on, so I can see it on you," I said. Ten minutes later she returned to the room and stood before me. "Sujin, I always want you to remember your Korean outfit. It represents your culture. Do not forget your motherland, like I shall never forget Vietnam." From time to time now, on special occasions, I encourage her to wear her Korean costume.

The time came for us to leave Korea and for Sujin to say good-bye to her sister. Surprisingly, they never hugged or kissed each other. They just chatted back and forth. I assumed that they were telling each other "take care of yourself. Have a good trip, and write sometimes." I shook the sister's hand and promised, "You don't worry about Sujin. I will love her and take care of her like she is my own daughter." I have kept that promise for the last six years.

We climbed into the Scout truck the army had provided for us to travel to the airport. As we rode along I reached out and held Sujin's hand. We looked at each other without saying a word and then turned away, each of us engrossed in our own thoughts. The view from Wonju to Seoul brought back memories of Vietnam. I know how Sujin felt at that moment, just as I felt seventeen years earlier when I left my motherland. The thought led me to create this poem in my mind:

> Motherland is poor but rich in nutrition;
> Mother's soul is wide as the ocean,
> Mother's love is high as the mountain,
> Mother's milk is always ready for her children.
> Motherland has a lot of fish to fry;
> In the field, there is a sweet potato vine
> For Yvonne to eat when the sun rises,
> Because it will help her brain be bright.
>
> Remember Mother when she is gone away,
> Gone far away into the silent land.
> Just remember Mother; we will understand
> For how much she has loved and cared.

When I was eight years old Jeannette and I would sit by the window every afternoon to watch the restaurant for our aunt. A very old man with no legs would often come by, begging for food. Tears rolled down my cheeks every time I saw the man. Jeannette and I usually handed him a bowl of rice with stew meat and then sat there and watched him eat, all the while feeling sorry for this unfortunate man. Whenever I was sad, I found myself writing poetry. This is the first poem I ever wrote:

Toi nhin len may toi hoi ong troi tai sao
Ly do gi toi con song sot
Toi nhin xuong dia nguc toi hoi qui tai sao
Ly do gi toi khong bi lua thieu
Toi nhin tren tran gian toi hoi nguoi tai sao
Ly do gi toi phai di xin gao an
Co le toi phi bo tan gao kiep truoc
Xin tha toi de linh hon toi duoc giai thoat kiep sau
Nhu vay toi duoc tro lai tran gian la mot nguoi giau co
De biet rang toi khong phai la nguoi an may xin gao.

I look up in the sky; I ask God why.
What a reason for me to be alive.
I look down to hell; I ask the devil why.
What a reason for me not to burn by fire.
I look straight at the earth; I ask people why.
What a reason for me to beg for rice.
Maybe I have wasted a ton of rice in my last life.
Forgive me, so my soul can be released in my next life.
That way I can return to earth as a rich guy,
For I know I will no longer be a beggar for rice.

My mind was busy with the flashback to the past. I did not realize we were already at the entrance to the airport. I breathed much easier now. "This is it," I thought. "It has been six long months. Time to go home. I am broke, but we have gained an addition to our family." I even thought about one day giving Sujin, Chris, and their children the money to come back here for a visit. That way their children would know about their ancestors, their motherland, and also the memories of Wonju that still are stamped deeply into their parents' hearts from the Land of the Morning Calm.

Chapter 12

A Family's Chaos

It had been six long months since I last saw my mother, although I always called at least three times a week during our stay in Korea to check up on her.

When we arrived home, Sujin was impressed with the house. To her it was clean and pretty. Even though it was a good-sized house, it only had two bedrooms. I gave the children my bedroom and moved my desk and all my writing materials into the living room. The sofa became my temporary bed.

"Good morning, Mom," Sujin greeted me the next morning.

"Good morning. Coffee is already made if you want some." I pointed in the direction of the kitchen and the coffee pot. Trying to make conversation, I asked, "How was your first night in America?"

"It was OK," she replied, giving me a smile.

"Good morning, Mom," Chris said.

"Good morning, Chris. You both want some breakfast?"

"Yea, please, Mom," Chris answered, and I got up from the sofa to make omelets for us. As we sat around the table, Chris announced, "Sujin and I are planning to get married on the twentieth of June."

"But that is only thirteen days away!" I gasped. "All right," I said as I took a deep breath, "whatever you decide."

After breakfast I showed Sujin around the house. "Chris can take my car today and show you around Crystal River and the beach," I told her.

"Thank you, Mom."

"Tomorrow we must find Chris a vehicle." Several days later, we found exactly what he wanted—an expensive, sporty Datsun, and I helped him close the deal.

On June 20, Chris and Sujin married. We celebrated with a luncheon at the restaurant in Cedar Key. Afterward I handed the newlyweds enough money to cover all their expenses for their honeymoon at Daytona Beach.

Before long Chris found a job at Proline Boat Company in Crystal River. Chris and Sujin continued to live with us for almost a year. Everything seemed to be working just fine. I worked on my book whenever I could during the day and retired to the sofa at night. Sujin worked at a restaurant as a cook.

From the day Sujin set foot in America, I treated her like a daughter. I taught her much about life and explained what she might expect in the future. Her English improved every day. I sometimes warned her about people and how they might try to mislead her. She must just use her ability to know the difference. "Remember your culture," I said. "Respect, faithfulness, and loyalty is not old fashioned. That is how we were raised." I did not use my authority as a mother-in-law to preach to her. All I could do was to show her my open heart, full of love and caring.

Often we sat on the porch in the evenings and discussed what life would bring us.

"I live here with you and I see you take care of Grandma. It makes me yearn for my mother's love."

"Do you miss your mother?" I asked.

"I saw her one time when I was young. I really don't know much about her. I feel good every time I talk to you, Mom. You make everything sound good and easy."

"You will find out in life that everything might sound good and easy sometimes, but life is easy if only we know how to handle it and accept it. We have been born close to the earth we live in. Nature has set one task for each individual: to perform our duties well. There are products on the market that promise perfection. It is the same with life. It can be ours if only we purchase well."

"What do you mean, Mom?" Sujin asked. "I should respect someone because they are educated?"

"No," I said. "You don't respect someone solely because they are educated. There are some uneducated people that earn the respect as well. You don't have to be rich, famous, or powerful to become somebody. You are somebody because of what you are, not who you are. Any education is the key to opening the doors for a brighter future. The best kind of education I have found was through my life's experiences."

"I have learned a lot from you, Mom."

"I have to go prepare dinner for us."

Not long after that, Sujin and Chris found a house and moved just one-half mile away from us. Sujin told me that from time to time she really missed our discussions we had on the porch in the past. Chris helped Sujin find a decent car so she would have transportation when he had gone to work. Although she could not drive, Chris and I taught her. Before long Sujin passed her driver's test and became a licensed motorist.

With them living in their own home and more independent now, I could get back to work on my book and sleeping in my own bed. How I missed my comfortable bed, but I never complained to anyone. After all, I had offered them my bedroom;

they never asked for it. I just wanted to see everyone living peacefully together and being happy, the way life is supposed to be.

Soon after they moved into their own home, Chris lost his job. Sujin had also learned she was pregnant! I was always there for Sujin whenever she needed me, either for money or help around the house. She helped me when I needed her too, but very seldom did I ask. I told her that I did not count on her and Chris paying me back the money that I had spent on them. The only reward that Charlie and I expected, just like mothers and fathers everywhere, was to raise their children and see them happy. This world contains many parents who have worked and sacrificed for their children, but few children who would do the same for their parents.

Charlie was always there to help me with the kids too. Not only did he help but he also cared a great deal for them. Often we would give them money, even though we realized that it was the wrong thing to do, simply because we loved them.

The "No Name Storm" of March 1993 hit us hard, bringing record flooding and engulfing our house in water. Water was eighteen inches deep in our living room. I then unplugged all the appliances in the house and placed our possessions on the dining room table. I handed Sujin two pairs of socks, and I told her, "One pair is for you and give the other pair to Grandma."

We all had a big mess to clean up and extensive repairs to make. I did keep my manuscript and wrote most of the nights, some nights more than others, depending on how tired I was after a day of long, difficult labor.

Together Charlie and I cleaned up the house and made the needed repairs. We cut the ruined carpet into small pieces so we could pull the heavy, saturated strips out of the house and dispose of them. This job took us two days to finish, after which we had to clean the bare floors with bleach to disinfect them. Our bathroom was the worst. We had to use a jackhammer on the shower floor and then haul the heavy chunks of cement to the dump myself since Charlie was physically unable to help me. With that done, we had to hire a professional to install a new shower.

The walls came next. We had to cut the drywall from the floor up to four feet high throughout the house and replace it. Chris helped us with that. Charlie also had to replace all the electric receptacles. Since we had no electricity, we could not cook and therefore ate whatever we could, mostly sandwiches. Often I would daydream of steaming bowls of rice and vegetables or a hot cup of soup. While Charlie and I were breaking up the cement in the bathroom floor to replace the pipes one afternoon, I heard a car pull into the driveway. It was Chris bringing us our usual lunch of Subway sandwiches.

My day began at 6:00 a.m. when I got up to make coffee. One hour later I was busy, working until 7:00 each evening, when it became too dark to see what we were doing. Everything still felt damp. I put in thirteen hours of hard labor each day—not too bad for a forty-five-year-old woman. At night I stayed up after everyone else had gone to bed to write for a few hours.

During my lifetime I had experienced abuse, rape, war, hunger, sorrow, fire, frustration, and now a flood. I could not quit my writing. When the sun rises and sets, instead of feeling one day older, I felt one day closer to reaching my golden crown—my book.

It took us a couple of months to complete the repairs and move back into our home. How fortunate we are to live in a country in which others care and come to our aid. I am so grateful to Governor Lawton Chiles, FEMA, the American Red Cross, and the Salvation Army for all their help during this disaster.

Although we moved back into our home, the repairs were not yet completed. Several little jobs still required our attention.

However, the first thing I did was organize my desk again so I could write.

I continued to work on my book until two months later. That September my precious Samantha, our first grandchild, was born. Chris and I went into the delivery room with Sujin while she was in labor. I watched Sujin go through the pain and the different phases of childbirth as I held her back to give her support. I prayed to God, "Please give Sujin the strength to go through her ordeal, and make both mother and child healthy." As I witnessed this, I realized what all mothers go through—the pain and torn skin—to bring new life into this world. How can we not respect, love, and try to repay our mothers in some small way? Once again I wanted to tell Mother, "Thank you, Mom, for bringing me into this world and nursing me for thirteen months with your warm milk."

Mother had once told me that when she was pregnant with me all she wanted to eat was rice and steamed mackerel. When I first began eating solid food, she would feed me rice and fish, which I really enjoyed. When she fed me rice and meat, I did not eat as much, which surprised her. She had never seen anybody eat as much fish as I did.

After Samantha was cleaned up, I looked her over very carefully. She was tiny, but that was to be expected because both of her parents were small. I held her in my arms and wanted to tell her how special she was to me.

Chris gave Sujin a kiss. "You did a good job, honey," he said. Sujin gave him a smile and then reached out for my hand. "Thank you, Mom." I gave her a kiss on her forehead.

Chris and I changed our clothes, discarding the hospital garb they gave us on the chair inside the delivery room door. As we walked out of the room, Charlie and my mother met us in the hallway. Later on they got to see the baby once Sujin got moved to a regular hospital room.

The next day I returned to the hospital to bring Sujin and Samantha home. I stayed with her for a few days to help her with Samantha and the house. I also urged her to take good care of herself.

Chris had just been accepted into the pipe fitter's union. He was delighted and anxious to work during the day and attend school at night, although he had to drive five hours round trip every day. Sujin stayed home about two months with Samantha and then returned to her job at the restaurant. Mother and I sometimes watched Samantha. Other times, Sujin dropped her off at the daycare center.

I continued to work on my book every chance I got, and I took care of Charlie. All Charlie had to do every day was what Charlie wanted to do. Usually he'd wake up to coffee and breakfast. Then by 9:00 a.m. he'd be out fishing until 4:00 in the afternoon. When he got tired he would come home, take a bath, eat dinner, and relax in front of the television until bedtime at 10:00 p.m.

I had no objection to that. I was getting used to being alone. Many nights I would lie in bed, listening to the gentle rainfall. I felt like a flower adrift amid the water hyacinth, not knowing where I would end up. I felt like I died in the rain. I wanted to place my head in my lover's arms, close my eyes, and tell myself that tragedy is not the usual way of life on Earth. I remember when Charlie asked me to marry him on the plane in the danger zone. I promised him that I would love him, take care of him, and that he would breathe his last departing sigh in my arms.

The work on my book went on, although at times it was not easy to concentrate. Each day something else seemed to interfere with my work. Chris had recently decided to stay in St. Petersburg with his friends to save the cost and effort of driving back and forth each day. We all talked it over and decided it would be best for Sujin and Samantha to move in with my mother in the guest house, which was connected to the main house. That way we could save money on the rent. Charlie and I helped Sujin move. Even though the house belonged to me, I asked Mother's permission for Sujin to move in with her, because I respected my mother. Chris routinely came home once a week to see his family.

The house was peaceful, so I thought I would have a chance to finish my book. Charlie decided not to go fishing. I knew that if he did not want to fish something was wrong. When I questioned him, Charlie told me that he had not been feeling well lately. He got tired very easily.

"Let's go for a ride, honey," he said. "I want you to ride around the woods with me. We'll see something different for a change."

I wanted to make Charlie happy, so I went with him. We stopped and had breakfast along the road and then drove around Yankeetown and Inglis. We loved the woods and discovered several secluded properties for sale.

"What if we buy us a piece of property in the woods, so we can get away once in a while?" Charlie asked.

"I like the idea," I told him. "But we have to be careful. Plus, we just got done fixing our place because of the flood. Don't you think you should rest, Charlie?"

"That's all right. We will look and see what we can find." We continued to ride around until we saw a piece of property with three beautiful, huge oak trees and a house sitting back from the road. We drove in and looked around. I knocked on the door to see if anyone was home.

"The place looks vacant to me," I said.

"This is it, honey. I like it very much. This would be a quiet place for you to come and write."

"This is it. I like it too, especially those big oak trees."

We took the name and number off the real estate sign. Charlie said, "Why don't we just go to their office from here?"

"All right."

We drove to the real estate office to find out the details about this property. We wrote the contract that morning with our terms and our offer. We asked the real estate lady for a key so we could look at the inside of the house. We really liked the place.

She told us that she would let us know as soon as she contacted the owner. We waited almost a week. Our offer was accepted, which was good news and bad news. Again, I had to put my book away so I could help Charlie fix up the house the way we wanted. When we returned home, I wondered if I should tell Mother about the house. She was always afraid of the woods, the fear of Vietnam still with her.

When we first moved to Florida and bought the house in Ozello, Charlie was so happy because two sides of our property were on the water. Mother was frightened of the water and the woods. I felt sorry for her, so I never wanted to leave her there by herself. It was very difficult for me at the time, because I was attending real estate school and working.

Sometimes on the weekends Charlie took all of us out to dinner. Other times, he wanted only my company, which was normal in any marriage. On those occasions when we left Mother behind, I noticed, as we drove away, Mother sitting by the window looking out. I felt like someone had just ripped my heart out of my chest. I could not leave her and found myself making all sorts of excuses to Charlie so we could stay home. I would tell him I had a headache or an upset stomach.

Sometimes I watched TV with Mother for one hour in her bedroom, and then I'd come out to the living room and watch TV with Charlie for another hour.

Some people think that I am weak or stupid or that I don't

know how to enjoy life. I don't care. What is important to me is that I know how I feel and who I am.

I still did not know how I was going to break the news about our new house to Mother. I would find a way. The next day Charlie and I took Mother for a ride and stopped by the new house. The owner had given us permission to do whatever we wanted with the property, even though we would not close on the deal for another year. Surprisingly, Mother really liked it when we showed it to her told her that we bought it.

"Yvonne, I know for a fact that you wanted to live in the woods for a long time now. I think it is beautiful with the big trees. It is not really woods."

"Well, Mom, I am glad you like it. You will not have any problems here. You still have neighbors around you."

"I think after I live here a while, I will get used to it."

"That's right, Mom, and you will like it." I continued to show her around the outside of the house and the inside. "It has three bedrooms. I am going to make one bedroom for your living room and another bedroom for your bedroom."

"One bedroom is good enough," she said.

We spent the whole day there. At least it was a big relief for me that Mother was so willing to move into our new house. Charlie and I continued to work every day on our new place. I could only write a little bit at night when we returned home. Eventually we completely remodeled the house, putting in new carpet and wallpaper, painting, and building a screened-in porch. Ten to twelve hours were spent there each day.

Mother was happy for us and thought we got a great deal, but she said, "There goes the book again!" It was true, but I could not allow Charlie to do all the work by himself. I tried to do most of the work because of Charlie's age and his physical condition.

I didn't want him to do too much. I would rather he sit on the porch and drink coffee instead of working himself to death.

After a few months we completed the renovations. At this time a friend of Sujin's told her about the low-income housing in Crystal River. Sujin checked out one of the apartments, liked it, and decided to move in.

"This is it," I told myself. "I have to finish my book. No more kids and absolutely no more fixing up." I got back to work on my book again for a couple of months. Then one day Mother told me, "You should go to France to see your father."

I almost fell out of my chair. "This book is really a struggle."

"You can finish your book any time in your life, but you might not have another chance to see your father if you wait too long. Twenty-six years have gone by already," Mother said.

"That's right. I only saw him once."

"Get ready for your trip."

I took my mother's advice and called my father to let him know that I was coming to see him.

On October 5, 1995, my plane departed at 11:00 a.m. from New York City. From there I took Swiss Air to Geneva.

Chapter 13

THE REUNION

It had been twenty-six years since this métisse had seen her father. My tears and emotions came easily as I looked out the windows of the giant 747 setting down smoothly unto the runway at Geneva. The former French major, whom I had loved all my life without experiencing that close father-daughter relationship, and my brother Paul were to meet me at the airport. My sister Monique remained at home to prepare for the reunion. As the plane rolled onto the tarmac, I silently thanked God for this long-awaited moment when my father would once again hold me in his arms.

I was forty-seven years old, and it seemed as if my life had been compressed into that ten-minute walk to the baggage area and customs. Visitors were not allowed to this point, so I could not catch a glimpse of my father or Paul. With my baggage rolling along behind me, I arrived at the greeting area. The moment had finally arrived.

I spied Paul first because he was taller than my father. Then I saw Papa. After twenty-six years I found him again. Paul hugged me first, and I had to reach up high to hug him back. Then I hugged Papa, hoping this hug would reward me for all those years I had yearned for fatherly hugs. Although it is customary for the French to kiss one cheek then the other, I noticed that my father just kept kissing my one cheek. Finally he gave my other cheek a peck.

"How was your trip?" Paul asked as they led me to the car. As Paul placed my bags in the trunk, Papa opened the right rear door for me and then went around to the other side and got in beside me. Paul would drive us the thirty minutes to Saint Genis Pouilly in France.

"How is your mother?" Papa asked.

"She has asthma, sometimes severe. Some days are better than others," I replied.

Memories of my last trip to France in 1969 from Vietnam came flashing back. Saint Genis Pouilly had changed in twenty-six years. As we passed by my father's old house, I looked at the tall building with the words *Commerce Banque* that my father had sold for commercial use. Upstairs in that building was the room that had been my bedroom for one month during my visit in 1969. I remembered many nights when I would open the windows and look out at the majestic view of the Swiss mountains, missing my mother and Charlie. Many letters had been written to them from that bedroom; and the letters Charlie had written me in return with the English Leather fragrance I kept under my pillow, knowing that he was close to me.

We finally arrived at my sister's house. Monique ran out the door and said, "I'm so happy to see you."

"It has been twenty-six years. I'm so happy to see you, too," I said. We exchanged our kisses.

A lunch of steak, vegetables, and salad awaited us.

"Is your steak all right?" Monique asked.

"C'est très bon" (It is very good), I said.

We visited a little bit, and then Paul suggested, "You should rest and get ready for tonight. Let me show you to your room."

I excused myself and said, "Je te voir ce soir" (I'll see you tonight).

"À ce soir," Monique said.

Paul carried my suitcase upstairs for me and showed me my room, he then gave me a kiss and said, "See you tonight." Then he left.

It was a very neat bedroom with two large windows. I noticed a fresh bouquet of fragrant flowers on the table next to my bed with a little card that said:

> To Yvonne,
>
> Welcome to Saint Genis. Hope you enjoy yourself during your stay.
>
> Big Kiss,
>
> Monique

"It was nice," I thought, "and I will thank Monique when I see her tonight."

After organizing my clothes, I decided to take a short nap. I was exhausted from my long trip.

At 6:00 p.m. the rest of the family arrived home from work. My sister's husband and their children come from Geneva, and Monique's children, who were ages three and four on my last visit, were now close to thirty. They came and gave me hugs and kisses.

"Bon soir, Yvonne" (Good evening, Yvonne).

Paul served a special wine for the reunion and he made a toast. "Pour Yvonne et bonne santé" (For Yvonne and to good health).

Paul then turned to me and said, "I will give you three bottles of wine to take home with you to keep as souvenirs from our granduncle's wine business in Bordeaux." My elderly granduncle was still alive and well.

The dinner ended with cheesecake and coffee, served in a

warm atmosphere. A lot of questions and answers followed. The conversation centered mostly around my great-grandmother, who came from Italy to marry my great-grandfather. Italian law forced her to give up her family coat of arms when she married the Frenchman.

Monique pointed toward me and said, "He was like you, Yvonne. He liked to horse trade." Then she pointed her finger to a picture hanging on her wall. "Our great-grandfather painted that picture for his wife on her birthday."

When I admitted that I could paint too, Paul commented, "It is in the blood."

Everyone was very happy with this reunion. We all exchanged our life stories. I learned more about my family tree and roots. We finally exchanged hugs and kisses with a "Bonne nuit" (Good night).

I slept until seven o'clock the next morning. When I went downstairs I found Monique alone. Her husband and children had already left for work. The two of us enjoyed a quiet breakfast together of coffee and croissants. Papa arrived before lunch for a brief visit, and then we went on to Paul's house for lunch. Paul's home is located behind my father's old house, only two blocks from Monique's. They all lived here in Saint Genis.

Paul prepared a delicious meal of cold beef with crusty French bread, which we dipped into a cheese fondue. Afterwards Paul suggested that Papa and I take a tour of the town. I thought this was a great idea. I had yearned for the fatherly love for so long. My father and I went for a tour. When we passed by the old post office, my mind flashed back to 1969. I would walk from Papa's house to mail letters to Mother and Charlie in that post office. As we drove I asked Papa where Paulette was buried. My stepmother had died in 1973.

"Not too far from here," he replied. I asked him to stop by

the flower shop so I could buy flowers to take to the cemetery with us. We bought two bouquets—one for each of us to place on Paulette's grave. The cemetery was located next to the church. As I placed the flowers in front of Paulette's tomb, I said a little prayer of thanks to this generous lady who had helped my father find me.

Returning to Paul's house, Monique announced that she was ready to go home. We needed to prepare for our trip to the mountains the next day. As he dropped us off Papa gave each of us a kiss and left. "À bientôt" (See you soon).

The next day Monique and her husband, Pauland his wife Maryline, and I took a trip to Zermatt in the Swiss Alps. We left Saint Genis about 7:00 a.m. and drove through the city of Geneva, the international banking and diplomatic center. As we left Geneva we began to enjoy the lush landscapes and the hills and valleys. The varied Emmental, with its meadows and forests, reminded me of a peaceful paradise. The Emmental, located in Canton Berne, is in Switzerland's main farming area. The Appenzellerland is a green, hilly region that follows the line of the Alps through Eastern Switzerland. Its alternating ridges and ravines, forests and meadows are comparable with those of the Emmental in Canton Berne. Both regions produce world-famous cheese.

Several lakes caught our eyes during the trip, like Lake Thun, with a castle on its shore, and Lake Brienz, which stands in a delightful bay bordered by vineyards. Many beautiful mansions belonging to millionaires can be found along this valley. Château d'Oex is a favorite meeting place for hot-air balloonists. The trip to Zermatt is breathtaking and magnificent.

We stopped at a sidewalk restaurant for lunch, which consisted of pork loin cooked in a wine sauce, potatoes, vegetables, wine, coffee, cheese, and dessert. We arrived in Zermatt and checked into the Walliserhof Hotel in Tasch at half past six that evening. The hotel provided us with good hospitality, first-class cuisine, a guesthouse with all the amenities, and a quiet, relaxing atmosphere. Each room had a sun terrace, and the hotel contained a sauna, a lift (elevator), a spacious lounge, as well as a famous, rustic restaurant with a bar and charcoal grill.

After freshening up we went downstairs for dinner. When we got to the restaurant and sat down, Monique said, "There is the charcoal grill that they use to heat the cheese."

I looked where her finger pointed.

"Their house special is dried beef and fondue. What have you decided?" Paul asked.

"We will have their house special," Monique said.

The waiter brought each of us a tray of sliced bread, dried beef, pickles, and a hot baked potato in the middle. He then went to the grill to heat up the Raclette cheese. When he returned he put the warm cheese on each plate.

"It is very good," Monique said. She then went on and explained to me about the cheese—Raclette is the world's famous cheese used to prepare the fondue.

"It's very good," Paul said. "Do you and Yvonne want to order another plate?"

"Bien sûr!" (For sure!) I said.

After such a big dinner, Françoie (Monique's husband) rubbed his belly and said, "I don't need to eat tomorrow. I want to go to sleep, plus I am tired from driving all day today."

"I am ready to go to bed too. This colonel made me sleepy." (Colonel is a dish of lime ice cream mixed with vodka.) That was Maryline's favorite dessert.

"We have to walk to the train station to check the schedule for tomorrow's trip to the mountain," said Monique.

"I can't walk that far," Françoie said.

Monique then turned to Françoie and said, "You need to walk. Look at your belly."

We finally got up from the table and walked to the train station.

The next morning Monique knocked on my room and asked, "Bonjour. Are you ready to go?"

"I've been ready," I said. "What about Paul and Maryline?"

"They will meet us downstairs for breakfast."

We dressed for our trip and went downstairs and ate a hearty breakfast. Then we walked to the train station.

We boarded the train, which took us to cable cars that transported us to the top of the mountains.

"Look down there, Yvonne!" Paul pointed his finger. "Are you afraid?" he asked.

"No," I told Paul. "I used to travel with Charlie. When we looked down from the plane, most of the time we saw the smoke, either from the Americans bombing or from the Viet Cong shooting."

Françoise was busy with his video camera while we were enjoying the magnificent view looking down from the cable car. There were not enough words to describe it. We were at the top of the world-famous Matterhorn. I could envision sports fans skiing to their hearts' delight there. We got off the cable car and walked everywhere we were permitted to walk. Paul took lots of pictures of us.

By late afternoon we came down the mountain and shopped around Zermatt. We bought a few souvenirs. I purchased a book, which Paul offered to pay for. The girl who worked there asked him in French, "Why do you want to pay for it?"

"Because she is my sister," he replied.

The girl looked at him for a minute and then spoke again. "That is impossible, because she speaks English and you speak French."

Paul answered, "Our father traveled a lot." Everyone was amused at the response.

Before we returned to Saint Genis, we stopped at the sidewalk restaurant in Zermatt and had a delicious dinner of deer tenderloin cooked with grapes and walnuts in a wine sauce, served with potatoes and French bread. For dessert my family talked me into trying "The Colonel." That was fabulous. My face, however, did get a little red from the vodka.

Everyone enjoyed the trip. Some even fell asleep while riding back to Saint Genis.

"Good morning. Did you sleep good last night?" Monique asked me the next morning as I walked downstairs to have coffee with her.

"I slept good. Did you?"

"I almost overslept this morning," she replied.

Papa arrived at 9:00 a.m. to pick me up. I was supposed to spend the night at his house. He lived about thirty kilometers from Saint Genis. On the way he took me for a grand tour around the area in which he now resided. His mansion had the best view of the Alps.

Papa took me on a guided tour of his house. As we passed the bedrooms he pointed to the right and said, "This is my office. It is small, but has a big window. I can look out and see my garden."

I noticed there were pictures of the entire family at the end of the table next to his desk. Two of them were my pictures.

"I was a little thin," I said to Papa.

"Yes, you were. You are just right for your height now and still beautiful." He smiled. Papa took me down into the basement.

"This is my favorite place."

"You have your own wine cave. There are too many bottles of wine in here."

"Oh no. There is not enough." He pointed to the wine rack

and said, "I drink this first, and the others I save for special occasions. That's the French. We have to have *vin et fromage* (wine and cheese). I will give you one, and Paul will give you two bottles of wine to take home."

"Merci, Papa" (Thank you, Father).

We walked upstairs to the living room and sat in front of the fireplace. Papa pointed at the painting hanging above the fireplace and said, "Your grandfather painted that picture."

I looked at the painting. It was a ship. I felt sad because it reminded me of the departure of Captain Pouley in 1954. I remembered it was my first scar of emotions of separation, as well as preparing myself to face life as a métisse.

I looked at the painting again and said to Papa, "Grandfather painted good. A lot of details are in the painting."

"I roasted the chicken with tomato stuffing today before you came. I will just warm them up and we will be ready for dinner," Papa said.

"Can I help you with anything?" I asked.

"No, everything is ready." Papa took some cheese out of the refrigerator and sat it on the table.

"I would like for you to try some of this cheese." Then he opened a bottle of wine, poured it in a glass, and made a toast.

"Bonne santé" (Good health).

After I helped Papa with the dishes, we sat in front of the fireplace in the living room and visited. Neither of us talked much about any particular subject. Once in awhile I noticed that Papa looked at me for a few seconds. I could see in his eyes that he was proud and pleased with me.

The next morning Papa had croissants and coffee ready for us for breakfast. While we ate Papa said, "Monique and Paul will come and pick you up. The three of you are visiting Perouges today."

"Have you been there before?" I asked.

"No, I haven't, but I have heard that the town appears to have been founded by a Gallic colony and the coat of arms of the two are identical. Enthroned on its hill like a queen, Perouges has remained a perfect example of a city of the Middle Ages. It sounds very interesting," I said. "History always fascinates me."

Papa said, "I also heard numerous films have been shot there, including *The Three Musketeers*, and *Monsieur Vincent*. I think you will enjoy the visit."

By that time Monique and Paul arrived and joined us for coffee and croissants. We talked for a while and then Paul remarked, "We better get going."

Monique and I got up at the same time to give Papa a kiss and then rushed out to Paul, who was waiting in the car for us.

"How far is it from here to Perouges?" Monique asked.

"It is about 134 kilometers," Paul replied.

At the beginning of our tour we visited Rue des Princes. It is the Ostellerie du Vieux Perouges, a thirteenth-century house classed as a historical monument, as is the museum opposite it. The museum contains various old objects found in Perouges: hand looms, parchment, weapons, old furniture, and statues. The interior is perfectly restored in every detail, including the furniture.

Paul looked at the map and said, "Let's go down to the Rue des Rondes, but first I want to take some pictures of you and Monique in front of the building."

We walked down to the Rue des Rondes. "In the middle of the Place du Tilleul is the Tree of Liberty, planted on October 21, 1792," Paul explained.

"This is the east side. This is where one of the great settings of the film *Monsieur Vincent* was made," I said. "Papa told me."

We walked down to the south side and noticed the street had kept its old-time look with projecting roofs and central gutters.

Paul stopped and said, "Let me take a couple more pictures."

Then Monique said, "Why don't you stand here with Yvonne? I'll take some pictures of both of you."

Our next stop was the house of the sergeant of justice, completely preserved. On its ramparts was a round tower used as a prison.

On our way out we found the old well in the square, formerly the only drinking water in the city.

We covered all of Perouges in our visit.

"Let's go have lunch," Paul suggested.

"Where do you want to go eat?" Monique asked.

Paul then turned to me and asked, "Do you like frog legs, Yvonne?"

"Yes, very much," I replied.

Paul then suggested, "We'll go to L'eau de France restaurant, where they specialize in frog legs sautéed in garlic and parsley."

We arrived back in Saint Genis late that evening.

The next day Monique suggested, "Since the weather is nice today, why don't we have lunch in the flower garden?"

"Sounds good. I'll help you carry the food," I said.

During the relaxed meal, we talked a lot about our lives. She told me one thing she will always remember. One time when she was four years old she was in her father's office. She found a picture of a baby with a paddy hat on and she asked her father, "Who is this baby?"

"This is your little sister," her father said.

She also witnessed her mother closing her eyes before sunset and praying. Curious, she asked her mother, "What are you doing?"

"I am praying, and this prayer is for your little sister in Indochina," Paulette said.

Monique went on to tell me that her mother had told her this story before she passed away: "Your father was already on board the ship to Indochina when you were born and when your little sister was born, he was on his way back to France. He did not have a chance to see either of his daughters when they were born." She also said that before he left Indochina, he had asked his best friend to give his daughter the friend's last name, because he could not legally do it himself. Now I knew where the name "Roullain" came from.

I thought about my life. It was sad, but very interesting. I just smiled to myself. It is a good thing that I am a writer and papers and pencils are my friends. They share my thoughts and my pains. I could not sleep that night. I could hardly wait to finish my book when I returned home to the United States.

The next morning when I came downstairs, Monique looked at me. "You didn't sleep good last night, did you?"

"Not really."

"Papa has gone bird hunting this morning, and I am preparing rabbit cooked in wine for dinner tonight. You and I are going to Geneva today to shop for chocolate for you to take home with you." After we had our coffee and croissants, Paul stopped by and asked to join us. He also wanted to buy me some souvenirs to take back.

Geneva was filled with banks. Several of them were owned by Arabs, and everything was expensive. Paul took several pictures of us around Geneva and by the lakes. We stopped by a sidewalk café for refreshments and lunch. We returned to Saint Genis early so Monique would have enough time to prepare dinner.

The dinner was delicious as usual, but everyone went to bed early that night. I asked Monique to allow me to prepare a

Vietnamese meal for tomorrow, and she was delighted. The next morning she and I went to the Asian grocery to buy the items that I would need to prepare the meal. I fixed egg rolls, sweet and sour chicken, and noodles cooked with vegetables. The French really enjoyed the egg rolls dipped in fish sauce. Everyone raved over the food, including my nephew and his wife, who came by train from Paris to see me. It was a long trip for them, but they made all the effort to meet their aunt.

Papa's birthday was the next day. Monique told me that we were going to his house tomorrow to wish him a happy birthday and to give him his birthday gifts. After a brief visit at his house, we all went to La Chaumière restaurant. On the menu was duck, beef, escargot, salmon prepared in wine sauce, and cheese. The best wine was served for this special day. What made this birthday special was the fact that all three of Papa's children were there to celebrate with him. My father was very happy because we didn't know how soon we could be together again.

It was my last day there. I slept well the last night after coming home from Papa's birthday party. I began packing my suitcase. Paul brought me three bottles of wine and three bottles of champagne, well-packed so I could put them in my suitcase. He told me to drink the champagne, but to keep the wine as a souvenir, because it was owned by the family.

Monique was preparing a farewell dinner. When we got ready to sit down, Monique showed me where to sit. I noticed there was a small package on my plate

After the rest of the family was seated, Monique announced that this dinner was in my honor and they had a special gift for me. She instructed me to open it, which I did very slowly. I stared at the gift for a long time. It was a beautiful pen.

For a moment my feelings flashed back to when I was a child and I had a chance to go to the market. On the way I always stopped by the store and leaned my chin on the display case to stare at the Pilot pen. I started to save my money, and marked on the calendar each day for 320 days. "By that time I should have enough money saved to buy that pen," I calculated. Although I was only eight years old, I was determined that if I had enough patience I would get what I wanted. I wouldn't have any problems later on in life, whatever it might be.

Monique looked at me. "This pen is for you to autograph your book, and here is an extra box of refills." I thanked everyone as I looked at the Parker pen with the name "Yvonne" engraved on it.

Paul poured a glass of wine for everyone, and we all made a toast.

"Bonne santé" (Good health).

"Bon voyage for Yvonne tomorrow."

"Let us not wait another twenty-six years for another reunion," Paul said. "I might have to walk with the cane to the airport to pick you up, and we won't be able to make a toast, because I will be shaking too bad to hold the glass."

Everyone agreed. There was a brief moment of silence. Monique looked at me. "Can you tell us briefly about your life in Vietnam?"

I paused for a moment. "Yes," I replied. "Since tonight is our last night for this reunion, why not make it a special long night?" I took a sip of water and began with my story.

My story ended at the same time the cuckoo clock struck two times. Everyone got up from the table at the same time. "Bonne nuit" for the last time.

The next morning Papa, Paul, and Monique took me to the airport. My flight was scheduled to leave at 9:00 a.m. We didn't have much time to visit. I already decided that I would kiss my father last, so that way I could spend an extra moment with him.

I would never be able to have enough of the fatherly love that I needed all my life.

"Bon voyage! À bientôt, Yvonne."

When my plane started to take off, I looked out of the window seat to see the shadows of my three loved ones still waving their hands from the roof of the airport.

Chapter 14

God, Please Give Me Strength

I returned from France in October 1995. I continued to write, along with my usual chores. I had two houses to maintain and a mother, husband, son, and his family to take care of. Whenever someone needed something, they always knew who to see. "Mom can take care of it," they said.

By the following January Charlie had become ill, and his condition had gradually worsened. I grew very concerned about him and insisted he go to the doctor for a check-up.

In the meantime I tried to sell our old house in Crystal River. We were supposed to close on our new house in March, just two months away. Besides, Chris had been laid off from his job, and Mother's health was not great, due to her severe asthma.

In early January 1996 our second granddaughter, Amanda, was born. Again I was there for Chris and Sujin. Then in July while Charlie and I were sitting on the front porch, Charlie began breathing very hard and complained that his chest felt like someone was pressing on it. I rushed Charlie to the Veteran's Administration Hospital in Gainesville.

When we walked into the emergency room, they asked me to wait outside while they worked on him. I tried to be calm, but how can you be calm when you don't know what is going on with your husband? I wondered, "Is he still alive or not?"

After an hour passed, they finally came out and informed me that Charlie's condition was stable. I breathed easier and asked the nurse if I could see my husband. She escorted me into the emergency room. I walked over to his bed and planted a big kiss on his forehead. "Hang in there for your famous author," I kidded.

Charlie tried to smile. "OK, author."

The nurse asked me to go back to the waiting room.

Finally they brought Charlie out of the emergency room and checked him into another room on the fourth floor. I followed them up to the room, but I had to wait quite a while before we got a chance to talk to the doctor. Then all he would tell me was that Charlie would have to stay in the hospital so they could run tests because they were not sure what was causing Charlie's breathing problem.

I stayed with Charlie. Later that afternoon they gave him a blood transfusion. I stood by Charlie's bed, wanting to see everything they did to him. I also asked a lot of questions, because I was concerned that his body might reject the new blood. I was right. It wasn't ten minutes before Charlie's breathing became more labored and he turned blue.

"You better call the doctor," I said to the nurse.

As I waited for the doctor to arrive, the nurse checked Charlie's blood transfusion machine and then his pulse. My eyes never left Charlie's face. I watched every change and impression. Minutes later, the doctor came in and I felt a little relieved. However, I was still very concerned about Charlie. After the doctor checked Charlie she turned to me. "Mrs. Combs, Mr. Combs is doing fine. His pulse is normal."

"Thank you," I replied.

The doctor gave Charlie some medication. He seemed to be resting quietly, but that is when I really had to watch him closely. I didn't want him to rest too quietly. That scared me. By midnight the nurse returned to check on Charlie. She suggested I go to the waiting room, where I could rest comfortably for the night. She would inform me of any changes in Charlie's condition.

I went to the waiting room and sat down in a soft chair. I prayed for Charlie's good health and that God would give me the strength I needed to endure this ordeal. Many things kept racing through my mind, including my book and my dream of becoming a famous author. I also had to squeeze in the time to go home in the morning for fresh clothes and then on to the bank to arrange a loan for our new house. Since the owner had postponed the closing date until September, that gave us the extra time we needed. I always believed in God, knowing He would never give me more than I could handle, and He would be there whenever I needed Him.

I tiptoed back to the room to check on Charlie from time to time throughout the night. I could not sleep, but I was used to getting only a couple of hours of sleep each night. By morning, Charlie seemed to be feeling a little better, but he could not eat nor drink anything.

Every time he tried to swallow he would vomit it back up again. The doctor told me they would begin a series of tests on Charlie.

I went to Sujin's house to pick up Mother. I briefly told them what happened to Charlie. From there I went home to change clothes and then to the bank, post office, and a few other places for errands. I returned home for Mother, who went back with me to the hospital.

Charlie remained at the V.A. hospital for two weeks. After a series of tests, the doctors decided that Charlie needed valve replacement surgery on his heart. I was not too happy with the news, but if that was necessary to keep my husband alive, then we would do just that. The doctor wanted Charlie to have several teeth removed before his heart surgery. Silver fillings and bad teeth could affect the new heart valve.

I hoped the closing on our house would take place before Charlie's surgery. The bank had already set the date, but it was delayed because they needed a survey of the property. My philosophy is that I will not sit around waiting for anybody or anything to happen. I will make it happen. I didn't call the survey office. Instead, I went there in person and insisted that they fax the survey papers to the bank. After that I notified the bank that the survey papers were on the way.

When I got home a nurse from the hospital called. "Mrs. Combs, I'm Elaine calling from the hospital."

Nervously, I answered, "Yes?"

"Your husband wanted me to give you a call," she said, "and wish you a happy birthday for him because he just had all his teeth pulled out and cannot talk."

"Thank you very much! Please tell my husband I appreciate that, and I am on my way to see him."

As I hung up the phone I realized that the date was indeed July 15, and this was my birthday. "You have not yet had a happy birthday or a merry Christmas in forty-eight years," I told myself. "Why not wait until you are fifty-seven and make that the happiest one so that you can remember it for the rest of your life?" I started dreaming about my book again. "Will it be done in time for my fifty-seventh birthday? Why not?"

I fixed a light lunch for Mother and me and then left for Gainesville. When Charlie saw me he said, "Honey, the doctor said I could go home for a week and then return for my surgery."

I held his face in my hands. "That is wonderful. We missed

you at home. Fee-Fee too!" Fee-Fee was our dog. Since Charlie had been in the hospital she would just lay by Charlie's truck and looked down the road. I stayed with Charlie until he was discharged. Although he was weak he was happy to go home. I could understand why Charlie did not like hospitals. After he was liberated as a prisoner of war, he had spent more than a year in the hospital.

Fee-Fee was so happy to see her daddy. It was the first time I witnessed an animal's loyalty to its master. I let Charlie relax and did not discuss any business with him. Five days later I told Charlie about the closing on our new home, now that everything was taken care of. "You did it again, sweetie," he told me.

Charlie did not realize it, but I was very concerned about his surgery, scheduled for the following week. We finally closed the deal one day before Charlie's return to the hospital and his valve replacement surgery. Throughout my life it seems like everything has been one day before—I left Vietnam with Mother one day before communism took over and we left Korea with Sujin one day before Chris's tour of duty was over.

The next morning, I took Charlie back to the hospital. He had to check in one day before his surgery. I stayed with him all that day. "Go home, honey. Come back tomorrow," he said. I didn't say anything, but I didn't want to leave him either. I just sat there and held his hands as long as I could, afraid that I might lose someone so precious and important in my life. Every surgery involves a risk. Charlie was seventy-five years old, which I discussed in detail with the doctor.

I stayed with Charlie until almost dark before I went home. At home I sat out on the front porch, thinking of all the times Charlie and I sat out there together in the early morning drinking our coffee before he went fishing. How I missed Charlie! I prayed, "Please, God, don't take my husband away. Even though my marriage isn't great and I've slept by myself for nearly twenty years, the idea of losing someone I love is even worse."

I got up around 4:00 a.m. to get ready for my trip to the hospital. Mother went with me. When we arrived at the hospital Chris was already there with his father. I helped Charlie with his bath and got him ready like he was instructed to do. Charlie sat on the bed with me sitting next to him. Chris stood by the window, a few feet away. Mother was downstairs in the waiting room.

The nurse came into the room. "Are you ready to go, Mr. Combs?" she asked.

"I am ready," was Charlie's reply.

"Mr. Combs, we need to take your wedding band off before you go into surgery."

"What?" I asked. That hurt, because to me it was bad luck. A thought crossed my mind: "Could this be the end? No!"

Charlie could not remove his ring, because it was too tight.

"We might have to saw it off when we get into the operation room," the nurse stated matter-of-factly.

"No," I demanded. I found some tape and wrapped it around the ring. The tape was to prevent any contact with the electronic equipment in the operating room.

"That might do it," the nurse stated. "If they don't want it that way, they can cut it off."

I held Charlie in my arms, trying to be strong enough for the both of us, but I could not keep my tears from escaping and rolling down on his ancient cheeks. "Don't let your Indian ancestors be ashamed of you," I whispered in his ear. "I love you."

The nurse wheeled Charlie out of the room, and we followed as far as we were permitted. When she pushed him through the automatic double doors, the two of us joined my mother in the waiting room. Chris decided to go to the cafeteria for breakfast.

"Mom, do you want anything?" Chris asked.

"No, thank you."

We waited until 1:00 p.m. I began to worry. Six hours had passed since Charlie had entered the operating room. My mind frantically asked, "Why is it taking so long? Did something go wrong?" Question after question kept popping up.

Finally the doctor came in, but the only news he had was for someone else's wife. He told that woman that her husband's surgery went smoothly, but he had a problem with his kidneys. Hearing that, I thought about Charlie.

I asked, "What about my husband, Charlie Combs?"

"I am not your husband's surgical doctor," came the reply. "I don't know."

The longer I waited, the more upset I became and found myself pacing in front of those formidable double doors. I began thinking about Charlie and me back in 1969 when we were flying constantly into the danger zone during the Vietnamese War.

At about 3:30 p.m. the double doors burst open. A nurse was wheeling another patient out. I took a quick look at the unconscious person lying on the gurney as she quickly rolled him out toward the recovery room. It was Charlie. "Thank you, God," I prayed. "He made it!"

I quickly retreated back to the waiting room and announced to Chris and Mother that I had just seen Charlie. They were thrilled with the news. A few minutes later his doctor came in to let us know that the operation had been successful and that Charlie was doing fine. We would be allowed to see Charlie in about an hour, once they set him up in the recovery room.

That hour stretched into two. At 6:00 we were finally granted permission to see Charlie. Chris and I went first. Charlie was still asleep. So many tubes were hooked up to him, but I could still see that he was my husband. Chris walked over to the bed and gently lifted the blanket from his father's hand. "Mom, look. They didn't take the wedding band off his finger."

The white tape was still on his finger, hiding the ring from view. I was so happy. Charlie tried to talk to us, but the tube in his mouth would not allow him to talk. Still very groggy, he found it difficult to open his eyes. "Dad, Dad, are you feeling OK?" Chris asked. Charlie nodded slightly to let us know he was.

I gave Charlie a kiss on his forehead. Some of my tears of joy also fell on his forehead when I bent over to kiss him. "I will always be here, Charlie. We will walk the last mile together."

With that Chris and I left him and returned to the waiting room so Mother could also briefly visit with Charlie. She returned about ten minutes later. Since we all had such a long, tiring day, I insisted that everyone go home. Only I would stay with him. Chris argued that he should also stay once he brought us something to eat.

I silently sneaked back into Charlie's room to check on him. His nurse was very kind to Charlie and his family. She walked me out to the waiting room and showed me where I could find pillows to make my overnight stay more comfortable.

Charlie's recovery progressed well. He remained in the recovery room for two days, and was then moved to a private room where he convalesced for another week. Every day I drove back and forth from Inglis to Gainesville to spend the day with Charlie. When he was home once again and fully recovered, I promised myself I would then return to my book. "Please, God," I pleaded, "don't let anything else happen before I can finish this book."

When Charlie came home, he required much care. In addition to his heart surgery he also had his teeth removed, so I had to mash all Charlie's food. His legs also caused him a great deal of pain, and I had to make sure he kept them elevated. The surgeon had removed a vein from Charlie's leg to use for his heart bypass surgery. Add that to the fact that he had suffered from severe beriberi as a prisoner of war, which aggravated the problem. Each day, I had to give him five different medications at varying times of the day.

Charlie gradually recovered, and I returned to my book, often working until 2:00 a.m. By January 1997 Charlie was much better. He had resumed his daily fishing routine, even though he tired easily and sometimes forgot small things because of his heart surgery.

On May 17 Chris had a bad accident on the corner of Linda Street. Chris and Sujin were going into a turn with the four-wheeler when a wild hog jumped out in front of them. Chris immediately slammed on the brakes. The four-wheeler got off balance and lost control, throwing Chris twenty feet away on the road. After a couple of minutes, Chris called to Sujin. She informed Chris that she was a little scared but was perfectly all right. Chris then tried to get up but was unable to. He called on Sujin to assist him, but she was unable to. Chris stayed on the road while Sujin went for help.

It was fortunate that he couldn't move. When the medics arrived they discovered that his femur was broken in three places. He required immediate surgery on May 18 and ten days' hospitalization. The doctor had to insert a sixteen-inch titanium rod in his leg, and Chris spent several weeks walking with crutches. I either babysat so Sujin could be with Chris in the hospital, or I had to stay with Chris in the hospital. On July 8, Chris underwent another surgery to further correct his injury.

I felt like a big pole trying to support a roof so it didn't cave in on my family. "God, please give me strength," I prayed.

"Are you doing all right? Would you like another cup of coffee?" Charlie asked.

"No, not coffee. I'll take a glass of juice, please."

Charlie brought me a glass of orange juice and sat down next to me. I held Charlie's hand and said, "I'm so grateful that we are still together. We have been through a lot for the last thirty years. If our love wasn't strong, our marriage would be in jeopardy."

Charlie squeezed my hand and said, "I'm grateful that I have you. Although I had experienced many terrible and wondrous things in my life, none could be more terrible than my experiences of being a prisoner of war. I even lost all hope of ever seeing home again, but here I am—home—and I am still with you, the only woman that I have ever loved, and you are everything to me."

I placed my head on Charlie's chest. "I feel your pain! You just reminded me of the Vietnam War when you reminisced about your wartime experiences. I am a victim of war, so I fully understand the actions of war."

"I'm sorry, sweetie. I should not have brought that up," Charlie apologized.

"You should talk about it sometimes when you need to. That will help you to get it out of your mind. I like to share with you. The American MIA issue is still in my mind."

"I remember," Charlie added, "the destructions ranged from the death of an individual to the total annihilation of a city, like Hiroshima or Nagasaki, Japan. It tends to dull the senses of one who has experienced war up close and survived as a noncombatant. Entire libraries could be filled with the details of destruction of one war, such as Vietnam. Human beings should be smart enough to learn from history, but most just muddle through each day, going along with the crowd or general consensus. The psychological destruction alone to individuals is catastrophic."

"The other side is always the bad guy," I uttered. "Suppose for a moment the possibility of both sides being right or wrong. One thing is for sure—results are never long lasting in terms of changing the course of human experience about war."

Everyone should be concerned about the significance of war as a global social problem. War creates fear, which dehumanizes everyone everywhere to some extent, perhaps even laying the groundwork for the next war. Living under the constant fear of war causes mental instability in millions of people all over the world every single day.

The hopelessness of it is staggering, and yet one can look at the good side of it. The very threat of nuclear war has almost certainly been a deterrent of a major war for the past fifty years, perhaps the longest running time of global "peace" in history. "Little wars" like those in Korea and Vietnam were carefully calculated so as not to bring on global conflict with nuclear weapons. As they say, "Old men start wars, our young men fight them, and our children pay for them."

I have to look at the history of my former country, South Vietnam. The United States became concerned with the Domino Theory, hoping to save all of Vietnam from the clutches of the communists and create a free democratic society throughout the North and South. The United States did not understand Vietnam's two thousand years of history and how much cultural and spiritual opposition there would be to a democratic form of government.

Will the United States become involved in another war? Of course. Looking at the past just reminds me of what the future holds in store for us. The histories of the two countries are somewhat parallel. Only the circumstances and reasons are slightly varied. That in itself should give us the answer to the significance of global war as a social problem.

"It's almost dinnertime. What would you like for dinner tonight?" I asked, changing the subject.

"How about chicken casserole, like the one you fixed a couple of weeks ago? It was good."

"I'm going to get the chicken out and let it thaw right now." I got up from the sofa and started to walk into the house.

"Look who just drove into the driveway," called Charlie. "It's Sujin."

"Hi, Mom," Sujin remarked as she walked through the door.

"Hi, Grandma!" Samantha ran towards me and gave me a hug.

"How is my petite pichonnette (little sweet baby)?" I called Samantha *pichonnette* like my mother used to call me.

"I missed you, Grandma, and I would like to spend the night with you."

"I missed you too, and you can stay tonight."

Sujin started out the door, "I'll see you later, Mom. Bye, Samantha!"

Turning to Samantha, I asked, "How was school and what did you do?"

"We colored and sang some songs. My favorite song is *Frère Jacques*, the song that Great-Grandma taught me."

"I like that song too. I used to sing it when I was a kid. Can you sing to Grandma a Korean song?"

"I don't know."

"You ask your mommy to teach you a Korean song. Especially learn how to say 'How are you, Grandma?'"

"But Grandma, you are not Korean."

"This is for your grandma in Korea. It is my wish for you, Amanda, and your mommy and daddy to see her one day. You sit here and color. I have to prepare the chicken casserole for dinner. We'll talk more later."

"I'll draw you a picture."

"Sounds good."

After dinner, Samantha, Charlie, and I sat on the front porch. We talked and played with Samantha. I held her in my arms and told her, "You are so precious. I love you."

"I love you very much too, Grandma." Then she pointed her finger to my forehead and asked, "Why do you have this scar right here, Grandma?"

"I've had this scar since I was six," was my answer. "One day when you are older, you can read Grandma's book. Then you'll know why."

"Did you finish your book?"

"I'm at the end of it; and I have promised myself when I finish writing the last word of this book, I will hold one piaster and fifty-seven cents in my hand once again and say to myself, 'Struggle is the mother of success.' I have kept one Vietnamese piaster since 1958 to remind me of the three hundred and twenty days that I had to save for my first Pilot pen. Those gifts are very sentimental, because they remind me of a child long ago who had a dream and struggled to become a 'famous author.'"

"Can you give me those gifts one day, Grandma?"

"Only if you earn them."

Chapter 15

MOTHER'S THIRTY-SIX DAYS OF FAITH

Mother went to be with the Lord on October 15, 1999. I am adding this chapter to my book to honor and remember my beloved mother Gioi Thi Truong, better known as "Mary."

Mother was diagnosed with stomach cancer in March 1999. "The operation went smoothly, but your mother is not cured. We found another spot that had already spread. She probably has a year or less," the doctor announced to me as he walked into the waiting room. The news hit me like a strong shockwave with both fright and denial. At the same time, I tried to pull myself together and deal with the reality. I prayed to God to give me strength to bounce back from this situation, which was causing me unbearable grief.

I went to the recovery room, put my face on Mother's stomach, and prayed, "Lord Jesus, please take all the pain from my mother."

"How am I going to tell Mother? And when?" I asked myself. What is her reaction going to be when she finds out she has cancer that cannot be cured? People's minds have a wonderful capacity for absorbing information only as they are ready to accept it. In the long run I have to tell her. I have to be open about the fears and hopes this sort of news brings, rather than trying to hide them. I must use the words and timing that I find comfortable in order to tell Mother.

I began a journey down a road paved with anxieties, hope, despair, sorrow, courage, and strength to define my own feelings and find my own ways of coping.

I stayed twenty-four hours a day for eight days with my mother in the hospital. When we returned home I put my bed beside hers and stayed with her constantly day and night to take care of her. Weeks turned into months. Mother would get really sick in her stomach. She kept vomiting, first solid foods, then liquids, and finally blood. The fact that she never had any pain made me thank God again and again for that blessing.

In September Mother got weaker. Each day I talked to Mother about God's creation: life, death, suffering, and salvation, while I rubbed her back and feet. I tried to be strong in front of her, but when she was sleeping or resting I would go out on the porch. My tears would roll down my cheek faster than I could wipe them away, and I would remind myself, "Be strong for Mother."

The Compazine medicine she was taking was supposed to keep her from vomiting, but it did not help. She could not even keep liquids down for ten minutes. As a result, she was beginning to feel tired and weak from not eating for so long. I knew Mother would not last long, so I approached the subject of baptism to her. Fortunately Mother agreed. I then called Sujin to contact our pastor, Dr. Peter Park. Shortly before he was due to arrive, I scrubbed the bathtub, dressed Mother in white clothes, and waited for the pastor to come.

Mother began vomiting constantly. Even though she was extremely out of breath, Mother suddenly made the statement, "'You need Me,' Jesus said."

At 7:00 p.m., Pastor Park, his wife, and friends came. We helped Mother to the bathroom and into the tub. Mother accepted Jesus for her salvation and she believed in him. On September 9, 1999, she was baptized. From that night on she was no longer afraid of death. She said, "I'm ready when Jesus is ready for me. The only thing I ask of God is to give me some time with my daughter to make sure she is strong enough before I go."

On September 12, the hospice nurses came. They were now checking on Mother twice a week. At this point Mom was constantly vomiting blood and losing weight rapidly. Sitting there next to her and watching her have to go through all this hurt me very much. I could neither eat nor sleep. I had lost twenty-two pounds in the last seven months.

On October 6 Mother became weaker and even more tired. She had only a couple of sips of water mixed with tea. She could no longer keep the smallest amount of liquid down, but her mind was still alert. "She has a very strong will," the hospice people told me.

I showed the hospice workers that I had given Mother nine different cards—Mother's Day, Valentine, birthday, Thanksgiving, Christmas, as well as a special note to thank her for carrying me for nine months and bringing me into this world. I also wrote a sympathy card to her, "Mother has just gone away on a pleasant journey. I am with you every step of the way. I miss you so much." Everyday I read these cards to Mother, like a little story; and she'd look at me and say, "You are a very devoted daughter. God will fulfill everything for you at the end."

She said, "Each year you gave me five hundred dollars for Valentine's Day, birthday, Mother's Day, Thanksgiving, and Christmas. Why don't you continue to do that? Then on July 15 open them all, take out the money, and go buy yourself something for your birthday from me."

"Mom," I replied in a small voice, "I already had that idea in my mind, but I will not open the envelope on July 15 to take the money out. That is for you, Mom. Instead I will keep that money in the envelope and help someone that needs it and tell them that it is from you to them."

She put her hand on my shoulder and said, "You are not only a devoted daughter, but also a true godly person. I'm so proud of you. I will die in peace. I will love and remember you forever."

The next day Mother made out several envelopes, placed two hundred dollars in each one, and addressed them "For Jesus." She gave some to friends to give to the church. I took her to drop off some herself. I was very happy with Mother's decision. She had little, but she gave it all to Jesus. That was the last trip she made with me on this earth.

On October 11 Mother was sitting up on the bed when she pointed her finger toward the window and said, "I see the cross. Oh Jesus, I wish I had a piece of watermelon now."

I told Mother that I would go get what she wished, but then a few minutes later a miracle happened. Miss Duck Yu, a friend, came to our house with a watermelon in her hand.

Mother said, "Thank You, Jesus, for granting my wish."

While I was cutting the watermelon, Duck Yu sang a song to my mother about Jesus in Korean.

It was the last meal my mother had on Earth.

My thanks to Duck Yu. She will always be remembered in my heart.

On October 13 Mother could not get out of bed. I tried to pick her up to set her on the toilet, but she was too weak to hold her body upright, which made her very heavy for me to pick up. I asked God to give me the strength to take care of my mother until her final breath.

"Yvonne," Mother called, "you have promised God that you will use the profit from your book to help the ones that need it. God will fulfill your dream—a struggling author." She shook her head and smiled, full of hope and promise when she said, "a struggling author."

On October 14 around 2:00 p.m., Mother's feet began to get cold. I was kneeling and holding her. I put my head on her stomach. I wanted to feel my mother. I wanted to smell my mother. The hospice people could not find her blood pressure or her pulse. Her system was already beginning to shut down. It was a miracle and she was blessed because she had no pain, for which we were truly grateful. I kept holding Mother. Although her eyes were closed, her mind was very alert. She mustered up all her strength to reach under her pillow and hand me a picture of Jesus. "You keep this picture, but you have to let me go, Yvonne. You go and pray to Jesus to take me. Remember what I have told you—your book will be successful. It's a witness through you and me that Jesus is with us. Jesus is with us," she repeated a couple of more times. Those were the very last words I heard from my mother.

I tried to control myself not to cry, but as soon as I got into the bathroom, I knelt in front of the tub in which Mother had been baptized and prayed. I cried to Jesus so much that day. All I could say was, "I have to let Mother go. She wants to go and she is waiting for You, Jesus." I returned and sat by my mother, holding her hands, and kissing her all over. Her eyes were still closed. I looked at the picture of Jesus that she had just given to me. She owned that picture since she first came to the United States. It went with her to the hospital; and on her return home it stayed under her pillow.

About 3:00 a.m. the next day, October 15, Jesus came while Mother was sleeping and said, "Gioi, follow me."

The sun has given the earth its final bath for Gioi Thi Truong, "Mary." I held my mother close to my heart and said, "How I wish this moment could last forever." I looked heavenward and said, "You are there, Mother."

God gave me time to mourn for my mother. I cried a lot. It was an overwhelming grief for me. I visited my mother's grave almost every day. I still bring her a cup of coffee in the morning, sit down, and drink with her. Before I eat anything I think of her first and ask silently, "Mom, please join me to share this food." I hug the place where she used to lie each morning and each night.

I have hung the picture of Jesus on the wall in the corner of my bedroom, where I prayed every morning and every night.

I would like to express a special thanks to all the people who sent me flowers, cards, and attended my mother's funeral service. I also wish to thank all of the American people for permitting my mother to drop her anchor on your golden shores before God gave her a permanent home in heaven. May God bless each and every one of you!

After I laid Mother to rest on October 18, I returned to the house, my eyes overflowing with tears. I already missed my mother. I endured my sorrow in the midst of my loneliness, but I was strong and determined, for I know God is with me. I went in and sat on the green chair in Mother's bedroom and prayed, asking God for the strength that I would need to continue to endure each sorrowful day. I missed my mother so much. Then I took her pillow and put it next to mine and covered myself with her blanket. I just wanted to smell my mother. I cried all day and all night. I was overwhelmed with grief.

On October 19 about 10:20 p.m., while I was lying in bed missing my mother I suddenly became aware of the light scent of Chantilly, Mother's favorite fragrance. I was so happy that I called out loud, "Mom, you are here!" I immediately jumped upright and tried to reach out and touch my mother, but she was not there, at least not physically. I heard no sound or voice, but felt a brief silent peace, as well as a message from God, "I will strengthen you."

With the power and glory from God, my strength gradually returned. I continued to visit my mother's grave at least three times a week. On each visit I brought a watermelon and placed it on her grave. I thanked God for giving her eternal life in heaven. I am so grateful for the love of Jesus. She is with Him forever. That is the reason I desired the gravestone to read, "Gioi Thi Truong, forever with Jesus."

I do miss my mother; I will see her one day. I have an important mission ahead of me. I always remembered what she told me three weeks before she passed away: "My devoted daughter, you have traveled two-thirds of the road of your rough journey. It may be rough on Earth, but it will be glory in heaven. You have to continue the other one-third in order for your journey to be complete. I thank you again for being such a devoted daughter. Remember your destiny is on earth, but your destination is heaven. Ma petite pichonnette, one-third of this road is all work that God has set for you, you will be successful." That conversation took place on September 26, 1999—the last time my mother called me *ma petite pichonette*.

On November 29, as I watered the orchid on my front porch, I looked at the flower and thought about God's creation. I thanked God again. In fact, I thank God every day for everything He has given us. "You have to make a testimony this Sunday in church," Jesus spoke to me, "I will guide you through it." This was the first time the Lord spoke to me. I was so excited that I threw the water bucket on the floor and walked into my mother's bedroom, which I now used for my prayers and writing. I knelt on the floor and prayed, listening for God's order, but nothing happened. I said to myself, "I will obey You, Lord."

Four days later on December 3, ten minutes past midnight, the Lord finally spoke to me. "You have to make a testimony about faith. Be obedient and thankful. You have witnessed your mother's faith in me. Now prove it to others. Tell them to be thankful for everything they have received from our Father in heaven." The message was clear. I went into my bedroom, picked up the phone, and called Pastor Park. I asked him to give me twenty minutes in church on Sunday morning. I did exactly as the Lord instructed me to do.

I returned to Mother's bedroom and sat on the green chair, trying to review in my mind what the Lord has said to me. The Lord left it up to me to prove to them. I knelt down and prayed again and again. Mother's face flashed in my mind. Jesus first spoke to her on September 9. While she was in the bathroom, ill and vomiting, He told her, "You need Me; you don't need medicine." Mother obeyed and had complete faith in Jesus for the remaining thirty-six days of her life.

I immediately changed clothes and went down to Publix to order a cake. I asked the lady in the bakery department if I could buy thirty-six little poinsettia flowers to put on the cake. "We don't usually sell them, but let me talk to the manager." A few minutes later, she returned. "We will give them to you. How many do you want?"

"Thirty-six," I replied.

After picking up the cake that Saturday I took the cake into Mother's bedroom, knelt down, and prayed to God. "Thank You, Lord, for giving me the opportunity to serve You." I then placed the cake on the table and started to decorate the cake with thirty-six poinsettias, which represented my mother's faith in Jesus for thirty-six days.

On Sunday, December 5, I took the cake to the church with me. Pastor Park called me up for me to give my testimony, as I had requested. After my testimony I then called for Judy Spradley, the youth Bible school teacher, and told her, "You did a great job with the children in church. Continue on doing your good work, because I believe that in order to see all the pretty flowers of our tomorrow the good seeds must be planted today." Next, I called for Natalie Mills, the church administrator. I gave her a gold broach. "Every time you wear this broach," I told her, "it will remind you of the job that you have done serving God by reaching out to comfort the elderly people when they are in need." I also thanked her for all the cards and visitations to my mother.

I closed my testimony by saying, "Have faith in Jesus and be thankful. Treat every day as a day of thanksgiving. The wheel of history cannot be turned back, but it is never too late for a new beginning on the right path. God loves you. He is waiting by your doorstep. Please invite Him in!" The song "I Surrender All" began playing.

I brought a piece of cake home and kept it in the freezer. That is my precious treasure. I also bought thirty-six white roses and placed them beneath the picture of Jesus in the corner of my bedroom, where I pray every morning and every night.

This chapter of my mother's life will never close. We shared too many memories of love, war, happiness, sadness, and sorrow during our fifty-one years together, and the most precious one was mother and daughter sharing a bowl of rice. Whether it was hot or cold it was a blessing to us.

I have had the following poem engraved on my mother's tombstone:

> Mother has gone on a pleasant journey.
> To live in hearts she leaves behind is not to die.
> There is a life above,
> And all that life is love.
> I love you "*beaucoup,*" Mom
>
> Ta petite pichonnette,
> Yvonne

Thank you, Mother, from the bottom of my heart for your great love and care. You loved me since I was conceived; you talked to me when I was still in your womb; you brought me into this world with joy on your face; you held me close to your heart with your warm hands; you looked at my face with your loving soul; you fed me with your mother's milk; you protected me under your wings; you washed my face with your gentle motions; you combed my hair with your loving care; and you kissed me with your tender lips.

You watched me grow up with joy in your heart; you taught me to be polite, disciplined, respectful, caring, and kind to others—especially elderly people. You also taught me to say healing words. Most of all, you taught me how to love by giving me all of your love. I will pass my love on to my children, my grandchildren, and my great-grandchildren.

Mother, I miss you. I miss your warm hugs, your kisses, your wonderful love, and your great care. Mother, I miss your loving face. I remember when I was in college in Saigon and you sat under the shade tree waiting for me to get out of the class and make sure I had a safe trip back to Bien Hoa.

Mother, cradle me in your arms once again to put me to sleep with the *j'attendrai* song. Mother, I miss your voice. How I wish I could hear your voice calling me once more, "Ma petite pichonnette, the fish and rice are ready."

Thank you, Lord, for guiding me each step of the way while writing this book. I am so blessed for the greatest gifts You have given me—those of giving, loving, and forgiving. I am grateful for all of the circumstances in my life, whatever they might have been. You were there to strengthen me and wipe thousands of my tears away.

I will always remember the first time I prayed when I was six years old, "Lord Jesus, please protect me." Thank

You, Lord, for protecting me all my life.

Thank You, Lord, for sealing me with Your Holy Spirit that lives in my heart. Thank You, Lord, for teaching me Your Word. Thank You, Lord, for giving me tremendous strength. It is a precious gift that I have received from Thee. Thank You, Lord, for giving me wisdom, making me the way You want me to be, and using me for Your glory.

O Lord, shine Thy light before us! For we need Thy guidance. We need Thy voice to direct us in our life. Help us to be strong in the face of temptation, strong in our love for others, and kind to one another. Teach us and our children to be thankful every day for what we have, instead of being upset for what we don't have. Teach our children to pray more often and honor their parents, Lord. Teach our children to respect the elderly people and reach out to help others.

Lord Jesus, I confess to You that I am a sinner. I repent of my sins. Please forgive my sins. Cleanse me as white as snow. Write my name in Your Book of Life. We are all sinners, Lord. Please forgive us all, and be with all of us to the end of time. We thank You, Lord, for healing all the sickness, taking all our sorrow away, and guiding us how to get along with one another in this world.

I thank You, Lord, again for giving me the chance to live and to learn many lessons in my life. In Jesus' name. Amen.

I learned to think with my emotions, spiritually-joined to deliver ideas that were practical and determined. I also learned that I can lose everything in life because of circumstances, but I shall not lose my dignity. My life lessons caused me to feel grief, but I must go on. I must put aside my feelings of grief.

I also came to realize that everything happens for a reason.

Therefore I cannot quit now. I must continue my struggle to achieve my goal. I am a persistent person. I am not giving up simply because I trust in God, knowing that God will be there to strengthen me.

Whether I am Yvonne or Métisse, I must get on with my life to reach out for a better future with my strong sheer force of my self-confidence, achieved through my long trial of sorrow.

I have learned many lessons through my journey of experience, and I know many more remain for me to learn—letting go of hurt, getting on with life, and forgiving those who hurt me.

> *I thank You, Lord, again with all my heart, my soul, and my strength for loving me. I love You, Lord, and You are my first priority in my life.*
>
> *In six more years I will be fifty-seven years old. I came to the United States with only fifty-seven cents. You said that number fifty-seven would mean something later on in my life. Only You know, Lord!*

My mother's baby girl has reached the destination that she always dreamed of. One dream has ended; another has just begun.

There is a wealth of knowledge that I would like to pass on to my son, Christopher, and my granddaughters, Samantha, Amanda, and Vanessa, as well as the readers of this book. There are all sorts of important lessons I have learned through my journey of experience that might aid you in your future.

I would like to tell you that you can do all things through Christ's strength. Do not blame anybody else for your own failures. There is always a price to be paid for success, as well as for ignorance and stupidity. We are what we want to become, and there are no excuses in life. The excuses are numerous, ingenious, and varied.

We must strike a precarious balance between our two needs—the need to be independent and the need for support. Balancing the tension is sometimes a painful process and one that is never completed. We must continually find our balance. There is a good deal of pain, as well as joy, mingled with our relationship with others. The strong, silent type seems to be impressive and self-sufficient. We might suspect that we would avoid most suffering and inconvenience if we could become that kind of person. To do so we would need to suppress something real and precious in our human nature. Enjoy the human element, that is, the growing feeling of belonging to a group from many walks of life, joining together for a common goal. Everyone likes a winner!

Be careful with whom you associate. You will become a part of what you are around. Value yourself. Even though in today's complex world nothing comes cheap in the real value. Be all that God has created you to be.

Believe in yourself, and nobody can make you feel inferior without your permission.

Help others. Respect the elderly people, give them a hand, and open the doors for them. Feed the poor. A piece of bread is worth more when you are hungry than a loaf when you are full. Be generous and kind to people. Speak healing words.

Honor your parents, because without them you are like a tree without roots. Let your parents know where you are so they won't worry. Regardless of your relationship with your parents, you'll miss them when they're gone from your life. Pick up the phone and call them. It is true that it is a parent's responsibility to take care of the children, but it is also the children's responsibility for what they want to become. We should not blame our parents' circumstances for our own failure in life.

Love and take care of your children. Do not abandon them, because the opportunity to multiply and bear fruit is precious gift that God has bestowed on all parents. Remember you are the artist of your children's portrait.

Take responsibility for your life experience, because your actions and reactions to others create it. Finish what you start. Do what you are supposed to do. Don't procrastinate.

Don't let your present circumstances determine your destiny.

If you define yourself, you have to set your limit.

Don't quit, because you never can tell how close you are. When the door of opportunity is closed, God opens another one—a better one. Seek God for guidance, for He is in control of our lives.

Learn to forgive yourself as well as others. Don't dwell on your mistakes; learn from them. Forget and go on. Realize that life takes place only in the present; the past is dead; the future only imagined. Fantasy can become reality. If you can dream it, you can certainly do it. Life is ongoing education, and you only get out of it what you put into it. Everything can come true in this promised land of ours. We can also become rich or famous without hurting or tarnishing other people's reputations. The door of opportunity is open to anyone that wants it, and wants it bad enough. With perseverance we can whet a piece of metal into a needle.

Grandma hopes that the knowledge that my mother passed on to me and that I now pass on to you and the generation to come will aid you through your life's journey.

Remember your grandmother gambled with fate and won her cherished dream. Grandma didn't give up hope and dream. It took Grandma fifty-seven years to achieve her goal of becoming an author.

Thank you one and all for sharing my journey. Because of you, I have had the chance to live once again through each episode of my life. I hope everyone will find some release in his or her life through relating to my journey of experience. Pain can be healed, anger and guilt can be erased, and problems can be solved. It all depends on our ability. It's all in our state of mind. Whenever problems arise, just think of all the pluses that you have had in life. Love, forgive, and have faith, first in God and then in yourself, even though in this age in which we currently live the press of a button could reduce centuries—in time as well as space, from east to west, and from the dim past to the urgent present. Let us keep the word *love* on our tongues and remain as intimate as ever.

I hope my many hours of labor will instill some knowledge into our younger generations so that they might understand the history behind the complexity of war and remember those who have fought so bravely with pride and honor for their country. May we not forget the MIAs in Southeast Asia.

On June 22, 2001, I stepped off the ramp at Ho Chi Minh City Airport after fleeing the war in Vietnam. My last *au revoir* (good-bye) to the country's two thousand years of war was on December 25, 1974, when I got my mother out of Vietnam just four months before the fall of Saigon.

It has been twenty-seven years, and many memories of war flashed back as I walked through the airport. The scars of the years have melted away. I suddenly realized that the soil of my motherland was under my feet once again. Emotions overwhelmed me. I wish my mother could be here to share this moment with me, as we shared many similar moments in the past—the most precious one being when we shared a single bowl of rice together in this land. My eyes were full of tears, and I said to myself, "I miss you, Mom, and I thank you for bringing me into this world."

After checking out of customs I walked out of the gate to the visiting area where a mob of relatives were yelling and cheering, "Chi Vonne, chi Vonne" (Cousin Yvonne, cousin Yvonne). They rushed with flowers to greet me. Many hugs and kisses were exchanged, and a few tears were wept along with pictures taken. My cousin Lan made the comment, "Lau qua, chi Vonne; con dep nhu xua" (It has been a long time, Cousin Yvonne. You are still as beautiful as ever).

We walked out of the airport and into a waiting van. My family never stopped talking all the way to Ho Chi Minh City, formerly Saigon.

Saigon has a new face since the war ended. I had a difficult time recognizing the places of my childhood. The law school where I attended classes is now occupied by the Vietnamese government. I was flabbergasted by all the new buildings, businesses, and very modern facilities.

We shortly arrived in Dong Nai Province, formerly Bien Hoa, where I was born and raised.

After a brief rest I went to a famous local restaurant on the river, where a welcome dinner had been arranged for me. Walking into the restaurant, I immediately noticed a big sign, "Welcome Home, Yvonne" and a long table adorned with flowers that stirred my emotions.

The dinner included all my favorite foods. This reunion reminded me of the one I had with my French relatives in France and Switzerland many years ago.

The next day we went to the market to visit other relatives and friends. They were so happy to see me again. They told me that they always remember me as a devoted daughter. Some of Mother's friends even delivered fruits to the hotel for me.

Before we went home I bought a sardine sandwich and I told Lan to take me to the Virgin Mary statue. It used to be my hiding place where I first found God's protection. There, I thought, "Lord, I am home!"

The following day I visited the local orphanage and the ward for handicapped children. They stayed in the church where I attended school when I was six years old. My heart reached out to them and the tears flowed freely. I donated a large amount of money to assist for their food and care. I also tried to find my former maid to help her with financial support so she could remodel her house. It took me three days to find her.

I had a chance to live once again each of the episodes of my life. Now is the time for *au'revoir* from my motherland and to come back to my homeland, the land of the free and the home of the brave.

I have closed the chapter in my life as far as the Vietnam portion is concerned and have started a new chapter in this promised land. I hope it is a long chapter, free of war and its consequences during my short residence on this tiny planet, so that every day I can say to myself, "Métisse, you are free. You are free."

I thank you for sharing this promised land with me. It is the same land that God has willed to us and to our children, now as well as the generations to come. He has given us the promised seeds. Now it is up to us to harvest them when they grow.

It is our duty to care for this land, even though it is a small part of the planet. We should give to it as though it were the whole world. We are the product of all those around us, and the fruits of our knowledge and labor should return this caring and sharing tenfold. One person can lift a stone, but it takes many people to move a mountain. Together we can make our journey through life richer and less steep, thereby allowing more people to reach their final destination. We shall continue to work shoulder to shoulder in order to keep the soul of America's promise so that our great-grandchildren might still have a chance to dance around the tree of liberty and dream of the America that generations of Americans have dreamed it to be. May we never forget our cherished moment on this blessed land and our noblest heritage of pride, freedom, and independence.

I am also proud of my Vietnamese heritage and will always preserve the values of the family's loyalty that I have brought with me from my motherland—the land that once upon a time held a French footprint and a beautiful love story that began but tragically ended with a *j'attendrai* song. However, the legend of the métisse lives on.

Whether we live in peace or in war, we should always keep God in our society, even though time has changed everything, including the human races of the world. With our modern technology and conveniences, we still do not have enough time for God, our loved ones, or to simply enjoy ourselves.

Yes, we are running out of time. We should wake up to our sins and live as though we are in the final chapter of our lives. We come from different backgrounds and take different paths in life, but with God, our spiritual beings are immortal, without beginning or end. Our Creator has scattered the seeds of truth over the centuries and over every continent of the earth.

Chapter 16

Come to Christ

On December 22, 2004, about 3:15 a.m., the state trooper showed up at my doorstep to deliver the news: "Mrs. Combs, you have lost your son. He was killed in an accident around 8:15 last night."

I was shocked, but I immediately thought of God and prayed for the strength that I would need to announce the news to my husband. I held on to the rail of the stairs and walked back upstairs. I came to my husband's bed. I held him and tried to comfort him, and finally I told him that our son was dead. My husband took the news real hard. He could not believe that our son was gone, and gone forever, from this earth. He left behind a father, a mother, an ex-wife, and three precious daughters—Samantha, Amanda, and Vanessa, ages eleven, eight, and four. Those innocent children are going to miss a lot of love and guidance from a father that has been taken away by a person that caused their father's death at the age of thirty-three.

At 7:30 a.m. on December 22, I called Samantha to let her know. I had prayed that God would give Samantha strength. It was the most painful call I have ever had to make in my life. God is a great God with His wonderful love and strength that He gave to Samantha.

December 26 was the day of the viewing. Samantha and I, followed by the rest of the family, walked toward the casket. It was an overwhelming grief. Again I prayed to God for strength. Samantha held me and said, "I cannot take it, Grandma." "Yes, you can, sweetie," I answered. "God strengthens you right now. We can do anything through Christ's strength in us. I believe it. That is why I chose the psalm for the memory service." Samantha looked up and told me with her broken voice, "Grandma, I believe it too. I feel better already." As I wiped her tears off I told her, "May God wipe all of your tears away."

We held on to each other for a long time. I have loved her so much since the first day she was born.

Samantha asked me, "Grandma, when you fear something, what do you do?"

"Keep telling yourself that God is with you and protecting you. If you swim in faith, then you will never sink in fear," I told her.

"That is what I'm doing now, and it works."

She is an exceptional child and a strong believer. She can write short stories and poems. We are so much alike. We are sensitive. Our hearts always pour out for others. Her daddy was the same way. He was very generous to those in need. I am so blessed and I thank God for giving me a son with a good heart and an exceptional granddaughter who believes in God.

My other two granddaughters tried to lean over the casket to kiss their daddy. Amanda kept touching her daddy's hair and said, "Daddy goes home. Daddy is with the cross." Vanessa tried to kiss her daddy again.

Monday, December 27 at 11:00 a.m. we were once again surrounded in the church. I was sitting there and looked at my only beloved child—a child that I gave birth to; a child that I used to cradle in my arms to put him to sleep; a child that I had raised from a good boy to a fine young man.

My beloved son, I never can love you enough. From the time you called me "Mommy," then "Mom" I was always there for you to share the joy, the sadness, your pain, and your burdens. My son Chris, your mom is still with you and will be with you forever. I will live once again with each of the memories that we have shared together. My mind flashed back to the times I used to take you to school in the morning and wait by the shade tree to pick you up in the afternoon. It was a joy to give you a hug and a kiss on your forehead.

On Sunday I watched you get on the bus to go to church full of joy on your face. I was so happy when you got baptized at the Baptist church in Homosassa Springs. You were eight years old.

Even though I was busy working, my family comes first, and my son is priority. I never missed once to take him to boy scouts, karate class, or baseball practice. He was very happy that his mother was participating in what he did. He joined the ROTC and was an expert marksman. Commander Labell and Chief Hudson were proud of him.

Mom and Dad were also proud of you. When you were seventeen you wanted to take flying lessons. I was very nervous the first time I watched you solo. I knew you were also nervous because it was the day that your instructor tore your shirt as a custom of the first solo. Not long after that you joined the army and was graduated from basic training and awarded soldier of the cycle. Major General James W. Wurman, Commanding General of Fort Dix, presented you with the certificate of achievement and bronze medallion. You were training in the army AH 64 Attack Helicopter Maintenance Program. After that you were sent to Korea.

After you got out of the army, you learned a new skill in civilian life. Five long years of welding school plus working. It was very hard for you, but you were determined to make it. You became a pipe fitter and welder. At the job they always requested a good welder by name, "Chris Combs." With those small hands God gave you to weld, you also used them to pray. I pray now that those hands will be used as a precious gift to wash Jesus' feet.

The memories of our last Thanksgiving together flashed back in my mind. We all sat together around the fire and roasted marshmallows. Vanessa lost a marshmallow. She looked at her daddy and asked, "Daddy, where did it go?"

"It fell in your sleeve, honey," Chris replied with a look of joy on his face.

"Mom and Dad, I thank you for this moment that we have spent together with the kids. I love you all very much. When I go back up north to work I will miss my family. I am so stressed out, and I miss my kids. I pray every night before I go to bed, "Lord, bless and give my parents a long life. I want to take care of them. Lord, watch over them and my kids. Lord, give me a family; I don't want to be alone." When is the Lord going to answer my prayers, Mom?" Chris asked.

"Be patient, son. He will. Sujin told me that you always pray before you go to bed."

"Mom and Dad, hang in there with me a little longer. I think next year, 2005, is going to be a great year. I thank both of you for the moral support and all the help and money that you gave to Sujin and me all of these years. And Mom, Sujin and I really thank you for sending us to Korea to visit her family."

"You are welcome, son. It was my wish for you, Sujin, and the kids to visit their motherland."

Chris was sad because he missed his family. He said, "I like her younger brother. I really had a good time with her brother-in-law when I first met Sujin. He and I used to drink soju. He beat me to it. Her sister really is a sweet person. I remember sleeping on the hospital floor with Sujin when her sister was there for her heart treatment. Even though Sujin and I were divorced, I was still concerned about her and I will always love her as the mother of my kids."

Chris reached out and hugged me as he told me, "Mom, I love you. You are a great mom. Thanks again for everything."

This was the Thanksgiving of 2004. Though it was the last Thanksgiving that we had together on Earth, we are together every day in spirit.

On December 19 Chris and his dad were standing by the stairway having a cigarette. He asked me as I walked down the stairs, "Mom, when is the Lord going to answer my prayers. I don't want to be alone anymore. I need a family. Pray for me, Mom."

"Son, have faith in the Lord and keep praying."

That night, about 11:00 p.m. Chris came upstairs and woke me up.

"Mom, I am heating up some egg rolls, and I would like for you to eat with me."

"OK, son," I said as I got up and walked to the dining room. As we sat at the table, Chris took the egg roll and dipped it in the fish sauce and put it in my mouth. He looked at me for a few seconds and said, "I want you and Dad to be happy. Take good care of yourself. Go have fun. I really love you, Mom. I am going to miss you all. Tell Sujin to take good care of my kids."

"I love you very much too, son. I will always be there for you."

On December 21 about 4:00 p.m. Chris went for a ride on his motorcycle. He came back with a friend named Tom. He introduced his friend to his dad. While I was picking up his clothes to wash them, Chris came up to me, gave me a big hug, and said,

"Bye, Mom. I love you. Bye, Mom. Are you going to say bye to your son?"

I looked at him and finally said, "Bye, Chris."

Chris then said bye one more time and told me, "Mom, you don't have to cook dinner tonight. I love you."

He walked out the door and gave his dad a hug and said, "I love you, Dad."

Then he left with Tom on the motorcycle. I looked at the clock; it was 5:00 p.m. It was the last time I saw my beloved son Chris.

I think of my son as often as my heart beats. I am sometimes looking for Chris to call or walk in the door with those familiar words: "Hi, Mom."

> My only beloved child, I miss you every day but will one day see you, because I know you'll be there waiting for me.
>
> You were hurting so much from missing your children due to your divorce. You were so heartbroken from being alone. You prayed to God to have a family again. Well, son, you are so blessed, for God loves you so much. He took all of your sorrow. He answered your prayer. He gave you a family of God full of joy, peace, and true happiness. All of us will be reunited one day. I thank God for giving you eternal life in heaven through your faith and acceptance of Jesus as your Savior. You are saved. I thank God for giving us the last 33 years together. It is not going to be easy for your mom, especially on Mother's Day. I have no more chance to neither give a Mother's Day card to my mother nor receive a Mother's Day card from my only son, but God is always there to strengthen me. Instead of sitting at home and feeling sorrowful, I will go and comfort those in

> sorrow, pass on God's love, speak the healing words, and be there for Sujin and my three precious granddaughters.

Brother Jake called Samantha up for her speech. Samantha decided to make a speech at the funeral service about her dad. I prayed to God to give her the strength to make it through the speech. I love her so much. This is Samantha's speech:

> Hello. My name is Samantha Yvonne Combs and my father is Christopher Addison Combs. He was a very good father, husband, son, and friend. He was a very good person. He always wanted what was best for me. My father meant very much to me. We had a lot of fun together. Even though sometimes he had no money, he did whatever he could for us.
>
> When I was small and my great-grandmother died, I did not know what death meant. All I knew was that she was gone. And now every time I think of her I cry, because I miss her very much. Missing someone is hard to deal with. And now I lost my father. The only people I have now are my mother and my grandparents. I knew my father was going to leave, but not so soon.
>
> He died at the age of thirty-three. I knew him for eleven years. On Tuesday, December 21, 2004, at 8:15 p.m. my father got hit on the motorcycle. I still can't believe he's gone. God has a time for everyone. My dad's time came early. He's in heaven now.
>
> I still remember the times when we would go fishing and would see who could catch the most fish. I also remember when we would sit on the swing together and not say one word to each other but would know what each other was thinking.

> I want my father to know that I love him very much, I miss him, and we are all a big happy family just the way he wanted.
>
> Even though some of you did not know my father, I thank you for coming. He's in heaven now. One day we will see him. He's always looking over us. He's always going to be taking care of us from heaven.
>
> Remember this, you never know how much someone means to you or how much you love them until they're gone. My father may have passed but memories will always be in my heart.

Samantha's speech was followed by the song "I Surrender All." This is the song Samantha and I sang to Jesus every time we were together. She and I decided to sing this song for her daddy. I decided on "Just as I Am," because I told my son when I died I would like for him to sing this song at my funeral, but he has gone first so I am going to sing this song to him.

As I sang I looked at my son lying there in the casket. I remembered that on December 19 he was standing in this church praying to God. He poured out his pain to God and confessed his sins to Jesus. I noticed he prayed for a long time.

After church that day Charlie, Chris, and I had lunch at Guy and Ohana's house. Ohana had prepared some barbequed ribs and some Mexican dishes. While Ohana was heating up the food, Charlie and Chris sat down with Guy and talked about all of Chris's accomplishments. Guy was especially impressed that Chris had flown his first solo at such an early age since Guy was a pilot also.

Lunch was served and it was very delicious. Ohana offered Chris another helping, but at first he was too shy to accept. Soon Chris felt at home and was helping himself to some more food. We were all laughing about that.

After lunch Ohana's daughter Aiko and Chris were talking about family and Chris had mentioned to her that he missed his little girls and that he was looking forward to seeing them for Christmas. Chris had told Aiko that family was the most important thing to him and that being with his daughters is what made him happy.

On December 21 he was with the Lord.

We were all touched by Samantha's speech and the songs we sang. I was so proud of her. A child with courage who believed in God is going to grow up along with her sisters without a father's love and guidance.

Only man should put the wedding band on the woman's hand according to God's plan. They became husband and wife and then father and mother. Together they brought the children into this world. Then they became a family. Let's keep the family together. I could hear from the distance the voice echo, "Mommy, Daddy, we need both of you. We don't want to grow up without one of you, and we don't want to hurt when we hang the light on the Christmas tree without Mommy's help or miss a gift from Daddy."

Chris already bought the Christmas gifts for his children this Christmas. From the next Christmas on I will make sure that there will be Christmas gifts under the Christmas tree for them from their daddy.

Have you hugged your children today? Tell them that Jesus loves them.

Chris's body was laid to rest next to his grandmother. His tombstone reads:

CHRISTOPHER ADDISON COMBS

March 26, 1971
December 21, 2004

Forever with Jesus

My father, you are in heaven now.
Now and forever I will love you.
Now and forever memories will be in my heart.
You are a good father.
We are so blessed to have a father like you.
I love you, Daddy. Samantha

Our only beloved son
Your weary soul no longer thirsts.
Nor are you sad or alone.
Dying with Jesus, by death reckoned mine,
Living with Jesus a new life divine.
One day we will be reunited
In family of God we will never be divided.
We are so proud to have a son like you.
We love you very much.

Mom, Dad, Susan, and the girls.

Thank you, Brother Jake, for leading Chris's funeral service. Again, thank you all for your sympathy and moral support during our time of loss. Your prayers, food, flowers, words of comfort, and presence were greatly appreciated.

My thanks to Ohana and her family, to Roy and Debbie Deweese, Kim Smith, Ronnie and Beth Lambert, Mary Jo and Jake Cravey, Nancy Holifield, Judy and Lee Childers, Rita Rains, and the Gooding family. I thank you for your love, your food, and your visitation.

On behalf of my son Chris, we wish to thank Mike Comber, Robert and Lori Young, Troy Rivera, and all the people from the union for your love and support.

My thanks also go to Robert Young, Troy Rivera, John Morris, and Felton who were pallbearers at my son's funeral.

To any friend that I have omitted, let me now acknowledge my debt.

May God forgive and bless the person who caused the accident that took my son's life. We forgive you. I don't want you to feel bad. I always put myself in other's shoes. If I feel that it hurts me, it probably hurts the other person too. That's why we need Christ in our lives to erase all of our mistakes and to comfort us and to bless us with peace.

I thank You, Lord, for giving me the time with my grandchildren. We had a great time together as always on their spring break. We refreshed some of our French conversation. We went to Fanning Spring to swim. Samantha made a comment while she was teaching Vanessa to swim, "If Daddy was here right now he could teach you to swim better than I can because he was the one that taught me how."

I knew Samantha wished that her daddy were here with them now. Chris was supposed to take Samantha to Six Flags in Ohio this summer. Samantha spent every summer with her daddy. They did a lot of things together. Sujin told me when I spent the night at her house that Chris did a lot of things with the kids; she also showed me the tape that Chris had made for her before they got divorced. When I was listening to the tape I hurt so much. This is part of what Chris had said in the tape: "Sujin, I tried to work hard to buy us a house. I am doing this for you and the kids. I want to be there one day with you when Samantha throws up her hat on graduation."

Samantha and I took Vanessa and Mandy back home. Samantha showed me a pair of shoes that her daddy had bought for her two years ago. She told me that even though the shoes were too small for her now she would like to keep them, because they were the last pair of shoes that her daddy had bought for her. I told her,

"Sweetie, this pair of shoes might be used as the picture for your book cover if you should decide to write a book one day."

She nodded, "I might, Grandma."

We went back to my house. Samantha spent extra time with me. I tried to do things with her to make up the difference that her daddy could have done for her. I encouraged her to do her best in life and to know that God has a plan for her and He will be there to guide her.

I know she will do well in school. In fact, she made the honor roll again this year. She also received the President's Award for Educational Excellence for being on the honor roll in the third, fourth, and fifth grade. Her daddy in heaven is so proud of her. I am also proud of her for what she has been through. She is doing great. She has read my book, and she told me, "Grandma, you are strong. If you can make it after what you have been through, then I can make it too. Grandma, what would you like for me to become?"

"It is not what Grandma wants, but what Samantha wants," I told her.

"I want to become a pediatrician, and I want fourteen kids."

"Fourteen kids?" I asked. "Don't you think that is more than you can handle?"

"No, Grandma. I want to adopt twelve, and two of them will be my own children. I want to take care of the orphaned and handicapped children. I will take care of Mandy too (Mandy is her handicapped sister). I have been helping Mommy take care of her and Vanessa."

"God bless your heart, sweetie. You will do well in life. Vanessa will too. Remember what Grandma told you: seek God for guidance in all you do in life. Give thanks to the Lord every day and keep praying.

"You saw Grandma pray every morning as soon as I arose and then I would pluck a flower from the garden to offer to the Lord. I pray again every night before I go to bed."

"I do pray every night before I go to bed, Grandma, just like Daddy did."

I reached out and held her tight in my arms and said to her, "Ma petite pichonnette, we are so blessed. God is shining the light in our house. We pray that God is shining the same light and is blessing others as well."

Thank you, Brother Mike, for baptizing Samantha on July 10, 2005.

May the Lord continue to bless you to carry on God's Word through prayer and baptism.

I thank God for bringing me to the First Baptist Church in Cross City. God has plans for me here.

Many lessons remain to be taught and learned. Much work remains to be done.

This will conclude fifty-six years of Yvonne's life. I finished this book in 1998. The book was not published because the Lord wanted me to live through two more chapters of my life. My beloved mother who gave me birth and my beloved son to whom I gave birth are both with the Lord. It's God's plan.

In the distance I still hear my youngest granddaughter Vanessa sing:

> Do I love Jesus deep down in my heart?
> Yes, I love Jesus deep down in my heart.

Her sister Samantha taught her this song. Every time they spent some time with me I always asked Vanessa to sing this song to me.

> My beloved son, I miss you and I want to tell you that Vanessa started school this year and every time Mandy sees the cross she says, "My daddy is with the cross."
>
> *Lord, I am so blessed that You used me for Your glory. I surrender all to You. May You be with all of us Lord who need You the most or the least. Through it all God continues to give us the strength we need to go on.*
>
> *Lord Jesus, we are all sinners. Please forgive us, Lord. We thank You Lord for dying on the cross for our sins.*

We're all part of the family of God and we are closer to our permanent home than we think. Do not delay. Please come to Christ. He is waiting for you at your doorstep. Please invite Him in. God has stood with His hand outstretched, not only to take you but also for you to take Him.

Thank you again for sharing my journey and permitting me to drop my anchor on your golden shores.

On behalf of myself and fellow immigrants to this country, I would like to express my thanks to all the presidents, leaders, and other Americans—especially the soldiers, those still living, as well as those who have joined their ancestors, for sacrificing their lives to defend and build this country. I thank you again for sharing this blessed land with me. I am so proud to be an American. I will always cherish the moment that I placed my right hand over my heart to be sworn in as an American citizen.

I thank you all again for giving me the chance to say to myself, "Métisse, you are free. You are free in America."

This poem I wrote is dedicated to the United States of America:

> I am pleased that I am a half-breed!
> I can see what my future might be!

From the distance, there is a liberty tree,
For I can see the half-breed dance free!
Love, forget, and forgive is life's key;
Work and achieve goals; depend on our ability,
For we are holding our own destiny.
From the distance there is a liberty tree.
Together let us keep this blessed land free,
For our children to harvest the promised seeds.

May God bless you and help you to have peace with one another. Don't give up hope—dream and be all that God has created you to be. Be patient! God does answer prayer.

Love and peace,
Yvonne

Epilogue

I enjoyed my most pleasant, tranquil feelings when I sat on the bank of the Suwannee River to write the last chapter of this book. The wind swept the marigold, dandelions, and the many other brightly colored wild flowers, making the woods burst with life. In the distance the shadows of boys meeting girls, which have haunted the pages of literature throughout the ages, made me feel lonely. If only you could look into the innermost depth of my soul and my spiritual eyes, you could see I was swallowed up by the sorrow of loneliness and that I yearned for love and to be loved. Most people will agree that love hurts sometimes. Yet without love, we are an incomplete, lonely mess.

In a few short months I shall turn fifty-seven years old. The planet is new to me again. For a long time now I have pondered the days of my youth. All of my youth's impressions are still strong within me as my eyes dim and wait for the end, playing out as vividly as my early life in that far-off time and place.

I have also learned that we can always reconstruct our lives, but first we must bury our sentiment of nonsense. It is never too late to purchase another ticket for the right destination.

My train is waiting for me. I must not delay. After all, I might not get there first, but at least I will not be the last one to accomplish the goals I have set for myself in this life.

The moon has beams!
The sun has rays!
People have destiny!
Destiny is what we make!